SCOTTISH WRITERS

Editor
DAVID DAICHES

ROBERT BURNS

DONALD A. LOW

SCOTTISH ACADEMIC PRESS

EDINBURGH

Published by
Scottish Academic Press Ltd.
33 Montgomery Street, Edinburgh EH7 5JX

First Published 1986
SBN 7073 0368 0

British Library Cataloguing in Publication Data

Low, Donald A.
    Robert Burns.—(Scottish writers; 8)
    1. Burns, Robert, *1759-1796*—Criticism and interpretation
      I. Title   II. Series
      821.6   PR4331

    ISBN 0-7073-0368-0

Printed in Great Britain by
Lindsay & Co. Ltd., Edinburgh

CONTENTS

ACKNOWLEDGMENTS

The award of a Leverhulme Research Grant in 1984 enabled me to complete research for this book. I wish to thank the Leverhulme Trust for this award; and also my wife Sheona, and David Daiches, for their helpfulness and practical encouragement.

CHAPTER 1

LIFE

Robert Burns was born in the Ayrshire village of Alloway, two miles south of the county town of Ayr, on 25 January 1759. His father, William Burnes, was a professional gardener who had come to Alloway from the north-east of Scotland. (The two syllable form of his name, corresponding to Kincardineshire pronunciation, gave way in due course to 'Burns' in Ayrshire.) Family tradition, which Robert was to accept, had it that the Burneses lost their tenancy of the farm of Clochanhill in Kincardineshire because they loyally shared the Jacobite views of their landlords, the Keiths, former Earls Marischal of Scotland. ('My Fathers', wrote Robert, 'rented land of the noble Kieths of Marshal, and had the honour to share their fate'.[1]) In 1748, William Burnes, and his brother Robert, a mason, left Kincardineshire for good. After a spell in Edinburgh, where he helped to lay out what is now an attractive public park, the Meadows, on the south side of the city, William Burnes found an opening as a nurseryman at Alloway, and in due course took a lease of seven and a half acres of land. There he built a two-roomed thatched cottage.

In December 1757 William Burnes married Agnes Broun, an attractive Ayrshire woman eleven years his junior. She had previously been engaged to a ploughman on her grandmother's farm near Kirkoswald. He proved unfaithful to her, so it is possible that she took up with the serious-minded William Burnes on the rebound. Agnes Burnes and her husband were well suited to each other, sharing firsthand knowledge of country things, and also a steady resolve to bring up their children in the Christian faith. William Burnes was a notably strict member of the Presbyterian Church of Scotland, while his wife belonged to a family and district which had been active in the proudly remembered heyday of the Scottish Covenanters. The Alloway cottage in which Robert spent his first half dozen years was a place of hard work and piety, in which the accent of Ayrshire mingled with what must have been a strong residual north-eastern Scots.

When his nursery project in Alloway failed to prosper, William Burnes became head gardener to a retired doctor called Fergusson, who owned the nearby estate of Doonholm. Having a kindly landlord and secure tenancy, it was natural for him to think in due course about adding the cultivation of a small farm to his work as gardener. It was just as well perhaps that the young couple were full of purpose, for a good deal of hardship lay ahead of them. William Burnes was a highly intelligent man, with the skill and independence of mind necessary in a farmer. He lacked capital, however, which meant that it was impossible for him to make the kind of investment needed to farm profitably. Given the deceptive hindsight of history, it can be argued that he might have done at least as well in the long run had he not made the move from gardening to tenant farming; but the lure of the farm was a potent one, and when in 1766 the opportunity came to take the tenancy of Mount Oliphant, some three miles from Alloway, he acted decisively. One factor which weighed with him was that, had the family remained in the Alloway cottage, in the years ahead it would have become necessary for him to put his children out to service, thus exposing them to unknown influences. A farm made it possible for them to remain under direct parental control.

Formal education had begun for Robert, and for his brother Gilbert, one year younger, even before the family moved from low-lying Alloway inland to the higher ground which gave Mount Oliphant its name. Generation after generation of Scots have seen education as the way forward in life. One of the ways in which William Burnes took his duties as a parent seriously had to do with book-learning. On a March day in 1765 he had interviewed at Ayr a young man called John Murdoch, whom he had requested to bring his writing-book with him. Murdoch was subsequently hired by Burnes and other parents in Alloway as a tutor for their children, living with the different families in turn, and imparting the elements of education, with the emphasis on writing, reading, and Scripture. He had a rather pedantic writing style, seen in his description many years later of the 'auld clay biggin' in which Burns was born at Alloway as the 'argillaceous fabric'; and he also formed the very curious impression that, when it came to music, 'Robert's ear was remarkably dull'; but despite his limitations, the poet's debt to him was real, in that he gave an introduction to the world of books. 'Robert, and his younger brother Gilbert', he wrote, 'had been grounded a little in English before they were put under my care. They both made a rapid progress in reading, and a tolerable progress in writing. In reading, dividing words into syllable by rule, spelling without the book, parsing sentences &c, Robert and Gilbert were generally at the upper end of the class, even when ranged with boys by far their seniors. The books most commonly used in the school were, the *Spelling Book*, the *New Testament,* the *Bible, Masson's Collection of Prose and Verse*, and Fisher's *English Grammar.* They committed to memory the hymns, and other poems of that collection, with uncommon facility. This facility was partly owing to the method pursued by their father and me in instructing them, which was, to make them thoroughly acquainted with the meaning of every word in each sentence that was to be committed to memory. . . .'[2] Murdoch's little school at Alloway — to which Robert and Gilbert walked from Mount Oliphant whenever they could — closed in

1768, and Murdoch subsequently moved to Ayr. However, he continued to visit the Burns household fairly regularly, and Robert took lessons in grammar and French from him as late as 1773. The year before, he and Gilbert had attended the parish school in the village of Dalrymple week about during the summer quarter, taking turns to stay at home and work on the farm. Thus their father's wish was carried out, and Robert grew up familiar with the written English word. Scots, though, was the language spoken every day in the fields, and whatever instruction Murdoch gave from books was easily matched in vividness and interest by the songs Burns learned from his mother, and by the stories of all kinds and, once again, songs, which he heard from her old kinswoman, Betty Davidson. The latter, he explained, 'had, I suppose, the largest collection in the county of tales and songs concerning devils, ghosts, fairies, brownies, witches, warlocks, spunkies, kelpies, elf-candles, dead-lights, wraiths, apparitions, cantraips, giants, inchanted towers, dragons and other trumpery'.[3] Betty Davidson and his mother were what modern folk-lorists would describe as 'tradition-bearers'. They provided him not only with incidents to send a shiver of fear down his spine or to cause him to laugh, but with a love of melody, a taste for an amusing story, and a sense of having been made the recipient in boyhood of a rich store of communally shared imaginative experience. As Burns put it himself, 'this cultivated the latent seeds of Poesy'.[4]

Although the Burns farm commanded attractive views of the coastal strip beneath it, life at Mount Oliphant often felt isolated in winter, and the farmwork imposed heavy demands on growing boys. Robert was to write feelingly of his teenage years there as a period which combined the 'cheerless gloom of the hermit with the unceasing moil of a galley slave'. After his death, his brother Gilbert supplied a more detailed account of the years of poverty which the family had to endure when their generous landlord died and was succeeded by a bullying factor who demanded arrears of rent. 'To the buffetings of misfortune', he wrote, 'we could only oppose hard labour, and the most rigid economy. We lived very sparingly. For several years butcher's meat was a stranger in the house, while all the members of the family exerted themselves to the utmost of their strength, and rather beyond it, in the labours of the farm. My brother, at the age of thirteen, assisted in threshing the crop of corn, and at fifteen was the principal labourer on the farm, for we had no hired servant, male or female. The anguish of mind we felt at our tender years, under these straits and difficulties was very great. To think of our father growing old (for he was now above fifty), broken down with the long-continued fatigues of his life, with a wife and five other children, and in a declining state of circumstances, these reflections produced in my brother's mind and mine sensations of the deepest distress. I doubt not but the hard labour and sorrow of this period of his life was in a great measure the cause of that depression of spirits with which Robert was so often afflicted through his whole life afterwards. At this time he was almost constantly afflicted in the evenings with a dull headache, which, at a future period of his life, was exchanged for a palpitation of his heart, and a threatening of fainting and suffocation in his bed, in the night time.'[5] It can be added that modern medical experts have accepted the view that over-work at this time probably caused permanent damage to Burns's heart.

But if he sometimes felt out of sorts, he was by nature resilient and quick to respond to any enlivening influence, whether in the form of a good tune, a joke, or a pretty girl. When he was fifteen, he wrote his first love-song, prompted by the presence of an attractive partner at harvest, Nelly Kilpatrick. She had a favourite reel tune and Robert made up a song to go with it, which survives. In later life, he liked to recall that love and the writing of verse entered his life simultaneously. From this time on, he was highly susceptible to female beauty. Two years later, his parents sent him to Kirkoswald, where he was able to stay with an uncle while studying 'mensuration' at a school in the village. His first protracted stay away from home offered unforeseen distractions. 'The contraband trade', he explained, 'was at that time very successful; scenes of swaggering riot and roaring dissipation were as yet new to me; and I was no enemy to social life. — Here, though I learned to look unconcernedly on a large tavern-bill, and mix without fear in a drunken squabble, yet I went on with a high hand in my Geometry; till the sun entered Virgo, a month which is always a carnival in my bosom; a charming Fillette, who lived next door to the school, overset my Trigonometry, and set me off in a Tangent from the sphere of my studies. . . . It was in vain to think of doing any more good at school. The remaining week I staid, I did nothing but craze the faculties of my soul about her, or steal out to meet with her; and the two last nights of my stay in the country, had sleep been a mortal sin, I was innocent. — '[6]

In 1777 William Burnes had completed his lease at Mount Oliphant, and given the family's lack of prospects and intense dislike of the factor, he naturally looked around for another tenancy. Finally he decided on a move at Whitsun some ten miles to the north, where he rented a farm called Lochlea, some 130 acres lying in a rather marshy depression almost midway between the upland villages of Tarbolton and Mauchline. The rent was high, a pound an acre; but the bargain struck with his landlord, David M'Lure, an Ayr merchant, produced for William Burnes what Robert described as 'a little ready money at the commencement; otherwise the affair would have been impracticable'. At first, indeed, the change proved to the family's benefit. Anxiety about money was temporarily removed, and it was stimulating for Robert, Gilbert, and their younger brothers and sisters to make new friends in the surrounding district. As usually happens with farming people, they probably made contact first with the sons and daughters of neighbouring farmers. A walk of two and a half miles, however, brought them to Tarbolton, with a population of some four hundred, and it became the focus of social interest in the years immediately ahead.

In 1779 Robert incurred his father's disapproval by attending a dancing class in the village. 'In my seventeenth year', he wrote, 'to give my manners a brush, I went to a Country dancing school. — My father had an unaccountable antipathy against these meetings, and my going was what to this hour I repent, in absolute defiance of his commands.' Sadly, his act of disobedience had a lasting effect on his relationship with his father. 'My father as I said before was the sport of strong passions; from that instance of rebellion he took a kind of dislike to me, which I believe was one cause of that dissipation which marked my future years. — I only say, Dissipation, comparative with the strictness and sobriety of Presbyterian country life; for though the will-o'-wisp meteors of thoughtless Whim were almost the sole lights of my path, yet early ingrained piety and virtue never failed to point me out the line of Innocence'.[7] The impression given by such records as survive from this period is of Robert's instinctive sociability and need to experience life being barely held in check by his somewhat repressive, prematurely tired father — and ready to break out whenever opportunity offered in further assertive self-expression.

Something William Burnes may have tolerated, rather than encouraged, was the formation in 1780 of a Tarbolton Bachelors' Club. Robert was very much the moving spirit behind this young man's debating society. The eighteenth century was a period when literary and social clubs of all kinds flourished. The Tarbolton Club, whose premises can still be visited in the village, was a distant cousin of such illustrious debating groups as the Speculative Society of Edinburgh University. The topics debated by its members were conventional enough, but some of the Club Rules show the influence of Burns's outgoing personality and social philosophy: 'No haughty, self-conceited person, who looks upon himself as superior to the rest of the club, and especially no mean-spirited worldly mortal, whose only will is to heap up money, shall upon any pretence whatever be admitted. In short, the proper person for this society is a cheerful, honest-hearted lad, who, if he has a friend that is true, and a mistress that is kind, and as much wealth as genteely to make both ends meet — is just as happy as this world can make him'.[8] It was also stipulated, with a touch of humour not always to the fore in such gatherings, that 'every man proper for a member . . . must be a professed lover of *one or more* of the female sex'. Burns, at least, had no difficulty in complying with this congenial requirement. The very first debate held by the Bachelors, on 11 November 1780, turned on a dilemma which was probably of his devising, if not yet within his actual experience. Its opposition between the claims of the heart and the head is very characteristic. 'Suppose a young man, bred a farmer, but without any fortune, has it in his power to marry either of two women, the one a girl of large fortune, but neither handsome in person nor agreeable in conversation, but who can manage the household affairs of a farm well enough; the other of them a girl every way agreeable, in person, conversation and behaviour, but without any fortune: which of them shall he choose?'[9]

Burns's social instinct found a further outlet through his entry into the masonic movement. He was admitted into the Freemasons' Lodge St David Tarbolton in July 1781, and became a committed mason, wholeheartedly sharing the philanthropic outlook and belief in friendship as a prime value in life of the 'brothers of the black tie'. His interest remained steady, despite a local split into two Tarbolton lodges. By 1784 he had risen to become deputy master of his lodge. Through freemasonry Burns got to know a wider circle of men than would otherwise have been aware of his existence. Among them was Gavin Hamilton, a lawyer in Mauchline who would one day be of great service to him.

The linen industry had made many fortunes in eighteenth-century Scotland, and remained profitable. Wishing to have some means of adding to the meagre returns which the farm provided, Robert and Gilbert Burns leased from their father a field in which they grew flax. In the summer of 1781 Robert moved to the coastal town of Irvine with a view to learning how to heckle the flax, that is process it for spinning. There he met and became intimate with a far-travelled sailor called Richard Brown. Brown, who was six years older than Burns, was brave, independent-minded, and magnanimous. Burns admired him intensely, and 'strove to imitate him'. But while it was Brown who gave Burns the first crucial encouragement he needed to think of publishing his poetry — ' 'twas actually this', Burns wrote to him, 'that gave me an idea of my own pieces which encouraged me to endeavour at the character of a Poet'[10] — in another way he set an example which the younger man came to regret. 'He was', Burns noted, 'the only man I ever saw, who was a greater fool than myself, when woman was the presiding star; but he spoke of a certain fashionable failing with levity, which hitherto I had regarded with horror. Here his friendship did me a mischief. . . .'[11]

Not only Burns's morals, but his health, suffered in Irvine. He experienced a spell of acute illness, making it necessary at one stage for his father to come down from Lochlea to help him over the crisis. When he felt unwell, his thoughts became sombre; a number of poems, including one entitled 'Prayer in the Prospect of Death', show how wretchedly ill he felt at this time in Irvine. Then to crown everything, his wish to set up in business as a flax-dresser proved completely unrealizable. He had entered into a business arrangement with a man called

Peacock, possibly a distant Ayrshire relative. Peacock
turned out to be thoroughly dishonest, either a receiver of
stolen goods or a smuggler. As if that were not enough,
fire destroyed all that constituted the flax-dressing experi-
ment during a New Year drinking party. Burns was to
recall the episode — caused, apparently, by the careless-
ness of Peacock's wife — with understandable bitterness:
'My Partner was a scoundrel of the first water, who made
money by the mystery of thieving; and to finish the whole,
while we were giving a welcome carousal to the New year,
our shop . . . was burnt to ashes, and left me, like a true
poet, not worth a sixpence'.[12] He returned to Lochlea a
sadder man.

His father, meanwhile, had fallen out with M'Lure, the
landlord. In the background of their soured relationship,
perhaps, was the failure of the Bank; the distress which
this caused was compounded for farmers by a series of
exceptionally severe winters. When rent from Lochlea
was not paid, M'Lure instigated legal action. On 17 May
1783 a Sheriff's officer appeared at the farm with a
warrant, and proceeded to 'sequestrate' cattle, crops, and
farm gear as surety against payment of rent. William
Burnes petitioned the Court of Session without success,
and the remaining months of his life were darkened by
anxiety and a sense of failure. Worn out by the struggle,
he died in February 1784, and was buried in Alloway
Churchyard. In his epitaph, his eldest son quoted
Goldsmith's words,

'Ev'n his failings lean'd to virtue's side'.

He wrote later to a friend, 'when my father died, his all
went among the rapacious hell-hounds that growl in the
kennel of justice.'[13]

Unknown to their father, Robert and Gilbert had
signed a lease with Gavin Hamilton to become his tenants
in the farm of Mossgiel, a mile or so to the east of the
village of Mauchline, which, with more than twice the

population of Tarbolton, stood at the busy meeting-point of six of Ayrshire's roads. Because steps had been taken to ensure that William Burnes's sons were properly recognized as employees of their father, they were treated as preferred creditors at the time of his bankruptcy, and by this means escaped prosecution. It must have been with feelings of relief, as well as sadness, that the Burns family — headed now by Robert and his mother — moved to Mossgiel in the early spring of 1784. The annual rent of ninety pounds for one hundred and eighteen acres was more favourable than that at Lochlea, and although the soil was heavy with clay, and the wind could blow shrilly at 600 feet above sea-level, prospects seemed good. Burns threw himself into his new responsibilities with vigour. 'I entered on this farm', he was to write, 'with a full resolution, ''Come, go to, I will be wise!'' — I read farming books; I calculated crops; I attended markets. . . .'[14]

At the same time, his life as poet, lover of women, and sardonic commentator on parish affairs entered a new, highly active phase. It was as if his father's death acted as a trigger, releasing a flood of creative energy through his being which demanded expression. He was now 'Rob Mossgiel', farmer and personality in his own right, and the world was going to know about it. In 1783 he had begun a private 'commonplace book', in which he entered, at first a little self-consciously, 'Observations, Hints, Songs, Scraps of Poetry &c. by Rob[t] Burness; a man who had little art in making money, and still less in keeping it; but was, however, a man of some sense, a great deal of honesty, and unbounded good-will to every creature rational or irrational'.[15] The notebook contains entries over the months from April 1783 to October 1785 on a variety of subjects ranging from Burns's wish to contribute to a body of poetry in praise of the beauty of his native Ayrshire — 'we have never had one Scotch Poet of any eminence, to make the fertile banks of Irvine, the romantic woodlands & sequestered scenes on Aire, and the healthy, mountainous source, & winding sweep of Doon emulate Tay, Forth, Ettrick, Tweed &c' — to the division of young men into two sorts, the 'Grave, and the Merry'. The latter, among whom Burns numbered himself, were 'the jovial lads who have too much fire & spirit to have any settled rule of action; but without much deliberation, follow the strong impulses of nature'. Full of literary and biographical interest though it is, however, the Commonplace Book was a means of recording his ideas which Burns outgrew even while making use of it. His nature craved direct communication with his fellow beings. He took to writing poems on the amusing side of life in the parish, and sent 'verse epistles' or letter-poems to other poets of the district, men like John Lapraik from Muirkirk, one of whose compositions Burns chanced to hear one evening at a 'rocking' or social gathering, and David Sillar, a neighbour from the Tarbolton days whose skill as a fiddler Burns admired. There were songs to tease the girls of Mauchline, daring satires on church affairs to amuse the bold and free spirits of the community, and deftly controlled socially descriptive poems like 'The Twa Dogs' which were among other things a safety-valve to help the poet get rid of the intense resentment he sometimes felt at the unequal distribution of wealth in society. 'I now began to be known in the neighbourhood as a maker of rhymes',[16] he wrote. Circulating in manuscript, some of Burns's poems won him a reputation for originality and cleverness, although inevitably his aptitude in lampoon and hard-hitting satire also created one or two enemies in Mauchline and the surrounding district.

In addition to the psychological liberation which his father's death had brought about, there was a more specifically literary stimulus motivating Burns at this period. He owed much to a recent forerunner in Scottish poetry, Robert Fergusson (1750-1774). 'Rhyme', he later explained, 'except some religious pieces which are in print, I had given up; but meeting with Fergusson's Scotch Poems, I strung my wildly-sounding rustic lyre with emulating vigour'.[17] The edition of Fergusson's poems which he used was one published in 1782. It seems likely that Burns made what was for him the vital discovery of the work of his fellow Scots poet — 'my elder brother in the Muse' — two years later, precisely when its effect was likely to be most crucial. Seldom can the poems of one individual have had such a salutary influence as a model on the poetic practice of another. There was no question of Burns being in any way inhibited by the achievement of his predecessor. Instead, in poem after poem he built on Fergusson's innovative example, in this way carrying forward and widening the range of vernacular Scots poetry.

Burns's personal circumstances always strongly affected his writing, and this was very much the case during 1785-6, in every way an astonishingly busy year. By the spring of 1786 he had decided to have his poems set up in 'guid black prent' by John Wilson, a Kilmarnock printer, and published by subscription. In the event, *Poems, Chiefly In The Scottish Dialect* appeared in an edition of six hundred and twelve copies in late July. Arguably, but for the scrapes Burns had got himself into, he would not have taken this all-important step. At any rate, he would not have had to contemplate turning his back on Scotland and emigrating to the West Indies, as, for some months in the summer of 1786, he did. He had fallen in love with and made pregnant a girl called Jean Armour, the daughter of a mason in Mauchline. It was not the first time Burns had got a girl into trouble, nor would it be the last; but on this occasion he remained emotionally committed, as did Jean. The couple obtained a simple signed document which in their own eyes was evidence of marriage. Unfortunately, Jean's parents took a very different view. James Armour had a fainting fit, then sent

his daughter to Paisley, where he and his wife hoped —
vainly, as things turned out — that she might take up
again with a more respectable suitor than the erratic poet-
farmer of Mossgiel. For his part, Burns reacted by
plunging for a time into 'all kinds of dissipation and riot'.
At the very time when his *Poems* were creating excitement
in Ayrshire and being passed eagerly from hand to hand,
he felt hounded through having to avoid hostile legal and
Kirk representatives stirred up by Armour, and was in a
state bordering on complete nervous exhaustion.

Burns had already given up his share of Mossgiel to his
brother Gilbert, and was intent, somewhat desperately,
on sailing to Jamaica. The next turn of events is best told
in his own words. 'I had for some time been sculking from
covert to covert under all the terrors of a Jail; as some ill-
advised, ungrateful people had uncoupled the merciless
legal Pack at my heels. — I had taken the last farewell of
my few friends; my chest was on the road to Greenock; I
had composed my last song I should ever measure in
Caledonia, ''The gloomy night is gathering fast'', when a
letter from Dr Blacklock to a friend of mine overthrew all
my schemes by rousing my poetic ambition. — The
Doctor belonged to a set of Critics for whose applause I
had not even dared to hope. — His idea that I would meet
with every encouragement for a second edition fired me
so much that away I posted to Edinburgh without a single
acquaintance in town, or a single letter of introduction in
my pocket.'[18] Seldom can any young poet have received
word about the fate of his poems with more intense
feelings of relief than the overwrought Burns. Thomas
Blacklock was a blind fellow poet and Ayrshireman,
prepared to exert himself on Burns's behalf. Soon,
Burns's work was being read by other influential men of
letters in the capital, where there was a network of men
from the west country. A number of prominent Edinburgh 'literati' showed Burns much kindness. The
admiration his work aroused was genuine; and along with

it went considerable excitement, as to superficial obser-
vers he seemed to conform remarkably to an idea which
was very fashionable at the time, that of the poet of genius
springing forth from a 'primitive' background and owing
nothing to learning. In fact, Burns was well-read both in
Scots and English: John Murdoch and his father had laid
the foundations, and he remained a voracious reader. He
was adroit enough, though, to do nothing obvious now to
destroy an image which helped to create a particular kind
of reputation for him in Edinburgh society. Robert
Anderson, a shrewd man of letters, commented later 'It
was, I know, a part of the machinery, as he called it, of his
poetical character to pass for an illiterate ploughman who
wrote from pure inspiration'.[19] One early review, in the
Lounger in December 1786 by Henry Mackenzie — author
of the sentimental novel, *The Man of Feeling*, which Burns
admired 'next to the Bible' — was especially influential.
Mackenzie applied to Burns the words 'this Heaven-
taught ploughman'.[20] Before long, the phrase was being
repeated in tributes which began to appear in other
journals, including a number of London publications.

Thus before the year was out Burns was well and truly
launched on the way to a phenomenal literary fame.
Farmers have a wry way which is all their own of assessing
a market. To his credit, Burns kept his head and his sense
of humour amid all the glare of publicity, writing ruefully
to Gavin Hamilton, 'For my own affairs, I am in a fair
way of becoming as eminent as Thomas a Kempis or John
Bunyan; and you may expect henceforth to see my birthday inserted among the wonderful events, in the Poor
Robin's and Aberdeen Almanacks, along with the black
Monday, & the battle of Bothwel Bridge. My Lord
Glencairn & the Dean of Faculty, Mr. H. Erskine, have
taken me under their wing; and by all probability I shall
soon be the tenth Worthy and the eighth Wise Man, of
the world'.[21] Among those who welcomed him most fervently were his fellow-masons, the Grand Lodge of Scot-

land toasting him in January 1787 as 'Caledonia's Bard'.
Characteristically, at the height of his success he remem-
bered the unhappy fate in Edinburgh of Robert
Fergusson, whose poems had helped to inspire his own,
and was instrumental in having a tombstone erected in
Fergusson's honour in the graveyard of the Canongate
Church.

Some impression of the poet's appearance and decisive
personality can be gleaned from the comments of obser-
vers who met him in the capital. Robert Anderson noted
that 'His dress was plain, but genteel, like that of a farmer
of the better sort: a dark-coloured coat, light-figured
waistcoat, shirt with ruffles at the breast, and boots, in
which he constantly visited and walked about the Town.
He wore his hair, which was black and thin, in a queue,
without powder . . . His behaviour was suitable to his
appearance: neither awkward, arrogant, nor affected, but
decent, dignified, and simple. In the midst of a large
company of ladies and gentlemen assembled to see him,
and attentive to his every look, word, and motion, he was
no way disconcerted, but seemed perfectly easy, unem-
barrassed, and unassuming'.[22] In 1828, when he himself
had known great fame and popularity, Sir Walter Scott
provided a personal reminiscence for his son-in-law John
Gibson Lockhart, author of the first biography of Burns.
'As for Burns, I may truly say, *Virgilium vidi tantum.* I was
a lad of fifteen in 1786-7, when he came first to Edinburgh, but had sense and feeling enough to be much
interested in his poetry, and would have given the world
to know him . . . I saw him one day at the late venerable
Professor Fergusson's, where there were several gentlemen of literary reputation, among whom I remember the
celebrated Mr Dugald Stewart. Of course we youngsters
sate silent, looked and listened . . . His person was
strong and robust: his manners rustic, not clownish; a sort
of dignified plainness and simplicity, which received part
of its effect perhaps from one's knowledge of his extra-

ordinary talents. His features are represented in Mr Nasmyth's picture, but to me it conveys the idea that they are diminished as if seen in perspective. I think his countenance was more massive than it looks in any of the portraits. I would have taken the poet, had I not known what he was, for a very sagacious country farmer of the old Scotch school — *i.e.* none of your modern agriculturists, who keep labourers for their drudgery, but the *douce gudeman* who held his own plough. There was a strong expression of sense and shrewdness in all his lineaments; the eye alone, I think, indicated the poetical character and temperament. It was large, and of a dark cast, and glowed (I say literally *glowed*) when he spoke with feeling or interest. I never saw such another eye in a human head, though I have seen the most distinguished men in my time.' To Scott, it appeared that Burns, 'having twenty times the abilities of Allan Ramsay and of Fergusson . . . talked of them with too much humility as his models'; and he added 'there was doubtless national predilection in his estimate'.[23]

The purpose for which Burns had come to Edinburgh was fulfilled in April 1787 when a second, much enlarged edition of his *Poems* was published by a subscription arranged through leading members of the Caledonian Hunt, an influential association of the nobility and gentry. Technically speaking, Burns was responsible once again for publishing the new edition, but after taking advice he had sold the copyright of his poems to William Creech, a notably stingy Edinburgh bookseller and printer, whose tightfistedness eventually left him feeling more than a little let down.

While Burns clearly remained his own man whatever the setting or company, there were inevitably days when he felt cast adrift from his moorings by the sheer speed with which everything had happened to him since the previous autumn. At such times, he turned away from the city's more elegant salons and drawing-rooms, seeking

out less sophisticated forms of companionship. Blacklock's friendly hint that literary success on a national scale
was in his grasp if he came to Edinburgh had been
followed by endless social encounters, including a succession of genteel attempts to advise him, lionise him, and
impress him with the trappings of city and university
culture. It was all fresh experience, and in that sense
welcome. 'At Edin[r]', he later commented, 'I was in a new
world: I mingled among many classes of men, but all of
them new to me; and I was all attention "to catch the
manners living as they rise" '.[24] In strictly literary terms,
however, Edinburgh was of limited value to Burns, at
least as far as the writing of poems was concerned. When
he was asked by John Ramsay of Ochtertyre whether the
Edinburgh Literati had mended his poems by their criticism, he was to reply, 'Sir, these gentlemen remind me of
some spinsters in my country, who spin their thread so
fine, that it is neither fit for weft or woof'.[25] A rather
stilted poetic 'Address to Edinburgh' shows that he
suffered a sense of strain through seeking to satisfy the
aspirations of some of his well-wishers in the capital.

Genuinely stimulating contacts he made in Edinburgh,
on the other hand, included those with individuals who
shared his collector's enthusiasm for traditional Scottish
songs and melodies. Since early in the century there had
been a movement afoot — at first little more than a fitful
and sporadic scholarly pursuit, but later a more widespread phenomenon, involving people from different
classes and backgrounds — to bring together whatever
from the past seemed to express Scotland's national
identity, including part of the country's rich heritage of
poetry, music and song. Antiquarianism of this patriotic
type had been given fresh energy and direction in Burns's
day by Enlightenment ideas about the value of intellectual
enquiry, working upon what many Scots felt to be a loss
of national pride and identity caused by the Union of
Parliaments in 1707. Mind and heart were both involved;

and it was this which appealed to Burns. For many years he had been attracted by the idea of gathering some of the old songs current in Ayrshire, and supplying words where need be to accompany the surviving old melodies. His Commonplace Book has the entry, 'There is a degree of wild irregularity in many of the compositions & Fragments which are daily sung . . . by my compeers, the common people — a certain happy arrangement of old Scotch syllables, & yet, very frequently, nothing, nor even *like* rhyme, or sameness of jingle at the ends of the lines. — This has made me sometimes imagine that perhaps, it might be possible for a Scotch Poet, with a nice, judicious ear, to set compositions to many of our most favorite airs, particularly that class of them mentioned above, independent of rhyme altogether — There is a noble Sublimity, a heart-melting tenderness in some of these ancient fragments, which show them to be the work of a masterly hand'.[26] Accordingly, when he met an unassuming music engraver called James Johnson in the spring of 1787 at an Edinburgh tavern get-together of a convivial society, and heard about Johnson's plan to collect and edit all the surviving songs of Scotland, he was immediately interested, and promised to do what he could to assist. Instinctively, he recognised that his artistic future lay as a writer and editor of the songs of the people, rather than with writing poems to please the *literati*.

After all his years of hardship and isolation, it is not surprising that at one level Burns was determined to make the most of the chance created by his modest literary earnings to take a prolonged break from farming and see something of life beyond Ayrshire. Thus, when his *Poems* were once more in print, he set off on a tour in the Borders. Two visits to the Highlands and one to Central Scotland were to follow later in the year.

His stated idea in travelling had to do with his aesthetic and patriotic feelings. Just as, when living in Ayrshire, he had felt a strong wish to respond to the beauty of the region, and to its history, now he was drawn to widen his experience, with the possibility of becoming, in the words of the masons, 'Caledonia's bard'. A letter to Mrs Dunlop of Dunlop of 22 March 1787 is explicit in describing his motives: 'I have no greater, no dearer aim than to have it in my power, unplagu'd with the routine of business, for which Heaven knows I am unfit enough, to make leisurely pilgrimages through Caledonia; to sit on the fields of her battles; to wander on the romantic banks of her rivers; and to muse by the stately tower of venerable ruins, once the honored abodes of her heroes.'[27] Interestingly, his immediate written accounts of his journeyings in Scotland — in the form of journals and letters — offer a rather different image of Burns on tour, at once more down-to-earth and less systematic in his approach. He jots down brief notes on the appearance of crops — rather than of landscapes — and assesses the character of the local farmers and the beauty of young women, instead of commenting in any detail on cultural history.

After his experiences in Edinburgh, Burns had no doubt hoped to travel with as little fuss being made of him as possible. This was not to be, however, for his name was now familiar to almost everyone with an interest in books. In the Border journal he comments amusingly, and at the same time perhaps a little wearily, on what it was like to be welcomed outside the capital as an author. At Dunbar he was taken to meet a certain Miss Clarke . . . 'a maiden, in the Scotch phrase, "Guid enough but no brent new", a clever woman, with tolerable pretensions to remark and wit; while Time had blown the blushing bud of bashful modesty into the full-bosomed flower of easy confidence — She wanted to see what sort of raree show an Author was; and to let him know that though Dunbar was but a little town yet it was not destitute of people of parts'.[28] Burns's travelling companion in the Borders was an Edinburgh law student called Bob Ainslie, whose family came from the Dunbar area. They naturally spent a fair amount of time in Berwickshire and the eastern part of the extensive Border country, crossing briefly into England for the first and last time in Burns's life. (On the way to Carlisle, the poet had 'a strange romantic adventure' with a girl who offered to take him 'for a Gretna-green affair' or elopement. Burns's response did not include marriage; therefore, 'finding herself un peu trompée in her man, she sheers off'.)[29]

In making such notes by the way, Burns was of course simply being true to himself. Yet the laconic and practical jottings in the diary of his Border tour, and the scarcely more detailed entries in his Highland diary, do not complete the account. He did in fact live up to his own aspirations as conveyed to Mrs Dunlop, but in ways which perhaps he had not fully anticipated before setting out on the road. A number of poems and songs were written straightaway; and more important, Burns laid in a store of vivid firsthand experiences of places, persons, and melodies. Expecially as a song-writer, he was to draw on the impressions and memories collected in this way for the rest of his life.

Each of Burns's tours had its own character. Perhaps because he wanted to visit the country from which a girl called Mary Campbell had come — 'Highland Mary', with whom he had a love-affair in the wake of the James Armour episode in 1786, had died tragically young — he travelled alone in late June from Glasgow to Arrochar and Inverarary. Less than two months later, he set out on the longest of his Highland sorties with William Nichol, an irascible, quick-witted Edinburgh schoolmaster (it was, said Burns, like 'travelling with a loaded blunder-buss at full cock'). Their route took them by Aberfeldy and Blair Atholl to Speyside and the north-east, where Burns met surviving members of his father's family. At Blair there was a pleasant meeting with Neil Gow, the leading fiddler of the day. Indeed, wherever he went in the Highlands he enjoyed new experiences related to his interests in music and song, including an encounter in Aberdeen with the son of Bishop John Skinner — who had written such outstanding Scottish songs as 'Tullochgorum', 'John o' Badenyon', and 'Ewie wi' the Crookit Horn'. The return journey to Edinburgh took in Dundee and Perth.

'The Birks of Aberfeldy', written at the scene in emulation of an older song from further north, 'The Birks of Abergeldie', and making use of its traditional melody, illustrates that the artistic stimulus Burns found through travelling was sometimes immediate. When, on the other hand, he toured with Dr James Adair, a fellow Ayrshireman, in Stirlingshire in October and visited the scene of the battle of Bannockburn, Burns's patriotic impulses were stirred at a level which was to produce its most memorable result only after many years had passed. In 1793 he would write 'Scots, wha hae wi' Wallace bled', to the old tune of *Hey tutti taiti*, on which he commented, 'I have met the tradition universally over Scotland, and particularly about Stirling, in the neighbourhood of the scene, that this air was *Robert Bruce's* march at the battle of *Bannockburn*.'[30] 1787 thus stands as a kind of watershed in Burns's life. He deliberately made use of the money he had earned to travel in Scotland, postponing the day when he would have to decide what employment to seek for the future; and — from the autumn, when he returned to Edinburgh — he threw himself energetically into songwriting and song-collecting for James Johnson.

On visiting Mauchline in June he had secretly seen Jean Armour again, with the result that she was once more pregnant. Eventually, he would marry her, and there would be a genuine setting aside of old scores between Burns and Jean's parents, but for the present — after they had made a show of welcoming Burns — relations remained problematic. For this reason among others, it suited Burns to be on his own for a second winter in Edinburgh. Already, however, he was thinking hard from time to time about what to do in the future. Farming was obviously one possibility, although he had taken too many knocks as a farmer to feel any real enthusiasm at the prospect. It had also been put to him that he might seek an opening to train for salaried employment as an Excise officer. The Excise seemed to offer a measure of security, and also a way of life in which with any luck there would be opportunities to get out and about and to meet people.

Before he had reached any firm decision on the question of employment, Burns once again fell heartily in love. The lady this time was a buxom Edinburgh 'grass widow' of almost his own age. Although still a married woman, Nancy McLehose had been forced to abandon her ne'er-do-weel husband. She wrote verse, and had a passionate nature, but was also possessed of religious scruples. After arranging for Burns to meet her and encouraging him to fall in love with her — which he duly did — she insisted on keeping the affair decidedly more platonic than he wanted. In the fashion of the time, if not perhaps of all of Edinburgh, the couple adopted the Arcadian names of 'Sylvander' and 'Clarinda', and proceeded to exchange a series of intimate letters expressing sentimental loyalty . . . and charged with ardour. Their meetings were occasions of strong mutual attraction censored by Nancy's conscience. She did not like Burns to speak about Jean. For his part, Burns was flattered that 'the Empress of his soul' was an educated middle-class woman.

Burns's frustrated desire for Nancy McLehose made him inform her that he was 'disgusted' with Jean Armour when he visited Mauchline in February 1788; but it was the unassuming country girl to whom he was to commit himself permanently. A matter of weeks after Jean had given birth to twins, both of whom she lost, a private marriage ceremony took place in Mauchline in April, probably in Gavin Hamilton's house. Thereafter, while there were to be a few letters and a poignant brief meeting in Edinburgh as late as 1791 between Burns and his Clarinda, she was forced to accept that he belonged to Jean. The unfulfilled love relationship, however, had clearly mattered intensely on both sides. When they parted, Burns sent to his mistress in Edinburgh perhaps the most famous of all his love lyrics, 'Ae fond kiss'. Then there is the evidence of an entry in Nancy's Journal for 6 December 1831: 'This day I can never forget. Parted with Burns, in the year 1791, never more to meet in this world. Oh, may we meet in Heaven!'[31]

The early spring of 1788 was a time of decision not only in Burns's personal relationships, but in his working life also. A well-connected friend, Patrick Miller of Dalswinton, had offered him the lease of Ellisland Farm, on the banks of the Nith some six miles north of Dumfries. Burns's first instinct was to fight shy of farming, with all the worries that it entailed; but after paying a visit to Ellisland along with an experienced farming friend of his father, he accepted Miller's offer. However, he also had it in mind to go forward with his plan to enter the Excise, thus covering himself against possible disaster. 'Don't accuse me of being fickle', he wrote to Clarinda. 'I have the two plans of life before me, and I wish to adopt the one most likely to procure me independence'.[32]

In the event, Burns's foresight in thus acting to secure a stable future for Jean and himself proved among the wisest decisions of his life. Miller had overestimated the quality of his land, and Burns found that Ellisland's attractive Nithsdale setting was in one sense a poor exchange for his recent lack of a permanent home: it was not at all an easy farm to turn towards profit. While a farmhouse for the family was being built — a symbolic action on Burns's part, recalling his father's commitment in Alloway — he ran into the first of many problems with the farm. It was a relief to him that his Excise commission was issued in July 1788, and that by September of the following year he was able to begin duty as an Excise officer.

In moving to Dumfriesshire, Burns inevitably lost regular contact with some of those he had got to know through spending many months in Edinburgh, as well as with his older Ayrshire friends. That he sometimes felt homesick, and disliked being cut off by the hills from his own county comes out in a number of ways in his writings. While he was waiting for his wife to join him, for instance, he wrote two wistful love-songs. The better-known one opens with the lines:

> Of a' the airts the wind can blaw,   directions   blow
>   I dearly like the West;
> For there the bony Lassie lives,
>   The Lassie I lo'e best: love
> There's wild-woods grow, and rivers row,   roll
>   And mony a hill between . . .   many

In 'O were I on Parnassus hill', he looks north towards the landmark hill of Corsincon, which can also be seen from near Mauchline, and writes:

> But Nith maun be my Muses well,   must
> My Muse maun be thy bonie sell;   self
> On Corsincon I'll glowr and spell,
>   And write how dear I love thee.

These, as Burns noted, were songs of his (interrupted) honeymoon, and in that sense not necessarily evidence of any sense of disorientation caused by the move south. One might equally conclude that a verse-epistle sent to Hugh Parker in Ayrshire shows no more than Burns's casually humorous way of expressing the irritations of the moment:

C

In this strange land, this uncouth clime,
A land unknown to prose or rhyme;
Where words ne'er crost the muse's
            heckles,
Nor limpet in poetic shackles;
A land that prose did never view it,
Except when drunk he stacher't thro' it;
Here, ambush'd by the chimla cheek,
Hid in an atmosphere of reek,
I hear a wheel thrum i' the neuk,
I hear it — for in vain I leuk. —
The red peat gleams, a fiery kernel,
Enhusked by a fog infernal:
Here, for my wonted rhyming raptures,
I sit and count my sins by chapters;
For life and spunk like ither Christians,
I'm dwindled down to mere existence,
Wi' nae converse but Gallowa' bodies,
Wi' nae kend face but Jenny Geddes.

Glosses (left margin):
staggered — Except when drunk he stacher't thro' it;
chimney — Here, ambush'd by the chimla cheek,
smoke — Hid in an atmosphere of reek,
hum corner — I hear a wheel thrum i' the neuk,
look — I hear it — for in vain I leuk. —
other — For life and spunk like ither Christians,
no persons — Wi' nae converse but Gallowa' bodies,
known — Wi' nae kend face but Jenny Geddes.

(Jenny Geddes was the trusty mare on whose back Burns had made his various journeys in the summer of 1787.) But while it would be a mistake to make too much of lines taken out of context, there is other evidence to show that Burns the poet felt acutely aware of having uprooted himself from his native county. In no sense had his poetic gift deserted him; but he now was separated by distance — and also by recent experience — from the cultural matrix of the Kilmarnock *Poems*. It was no accident that 'Tam o' Shanter', the most celebrated poem of the Ellisland period (which he was to describe wryly as his 'standard performance in the poetic line') was written out of a nostalgic and commemorative impulse, to recreate an Ayrshire story.

The full story of how 'Tam o' Shanter' came to be written belongs in a later chapter. Here, it is enough to mention that Burns at Ellisland had a kindly and prosperous neighbour of antiquarian tastes, Robert Riddell. Not only did Riddell introduce Burns to the gifted Englishman, Francis Grose, whose request for information about Alloway Kirk elicited 'Tam o'Shanter' in 1790. He made available to Burns a 'Hermitage' on his estate, where the poet was free to write when he chose; and he shared many of his intellectual pursuits, including the writing of notes on Scots song. Burns was deeply grateful to Riddell, compiling for his use the so-called Glenriddell manuscripts, copies of many of his letters and well-known poems. No single neighbour, however well-intentioned, could take the place of an intimately known rural community; but both as farmer and exciseman Burns mixed in varied society in Nithsdale. He was so busy trying to farm well, and covering his extensive Excise district on horseback, that very often there was little time left for the writing of poetry. His work on song, however, went forward steadily; for he had discovered many years before that tunes remained with him, and it was sometimes possible for him to draft songs in the fields or while riding from place to place. Something else which helped him as Johnson's collaborator on the *Scots Musical Museum* was the fact that Jean Armour was a natural singer with a good knowledge of the songs she had heard while growing up.

In the autumn of 1791 Burns renounced the lease of Ellisland. He had avoided disaster there, but lacked the capital to improve his land. Along with Jean and their growing family, he moved to Dumfries — having for the past year served full-time as an Excise officer in its Third Excise Division. In making the transition to town life, he took another important step, one which was to become very familiar as agricultural and industrial changes affected more and more lives. His final few years would see him still in touch with country people through his demanding rounds of duty as an Exciseman, but town-based. He had his own circle of friends in the busy market

town, and was a popular visitor at the Theatre and at the
Globe Tavern.

The early 1790s were a period of intense political
debate. Burns's essential sympathies were radical, but
indiscreet lines scribbled in Stirling about the Hanoverian
royal family in contrast to the Stuarts whom they dis-
placed had landed him in trouble early in his period with
the Excise; he therefore took care not to be caught out
expressing too much sympathy with the French Revolution. At a time when there was talk of the country being
attacked, he was indeed able, quite sincerely, to write
'Does haughty Gaul invasion threat?' for the Dumfries
Volunteers. Yet his underlying fellow-feeling with Tom
Paine's *Rights of Man* can be clearly seen in a song like 'Is
there for honest Poverty', in which his lifelong democratic
instinct merges with topical political sentiments.

Song-writing and collecting continued to the end. An
additional complication from September 1792 was that
Burns accepted an invitation to supply songs for a second
large-scale project, *A Select Collection of Scotish Airs*. The
man responsible for this was George Thomson, a committed and friendly but rather pretentious lover of
Scottish music, who considerably annoyed Burns at times
by suggesting that he should in his songs use English
diction — to appeal to polite taste — rather than the Scots
which he preferred. Predictably, Thomson received fewer
first-rate Burns songs than the unassuming James
Johnson. His main importance is that he drew forth from
the poet a series of eloquent letters about song in which
Burns vigorously defended his practice.

Work pressure was unremitting. Burns was clearly a
more than competent Exciseman, for in 1794 he was
appointed Acting Supervisor at Dumfries, a post he occu-
pied for several months while a colleague was ill. His own
health, however, was soon a cause for concern. Compounded by a rheumatic condition, the heart trouble
which he had suffered periodically since his early years of

overwork on Ayrshire farms returned to plague him. In the early summer of 1796 he wrote to James Johnson, 'This protracting, slow consuming illness which hangs over me, will, I doubt much, my ever dear friend, arrest my sun before he has well reached his middle carreer, & will turn over the Poet to far other & more important concerns than studying the brilliancy of Wit or the pathos of Sentiment'.[33] A young Highlander, James MacDonald, visiting Dumfries in the first week of June, noted in his diary that Burns looked consumptive, adding '[he] was in excellent spirits, and displayed as much wit and humour in three hours time as any man I ever knew . . . At parting the poor Poet with tears in his Eyes took an affectionate leave of me. He has vast pathos in his voice, and as he himself says in his Vision, ''His eye e'en turned on empty space, beams keen wi' honour.'''[34] At the beginning of July, Burns went to Brow Well on the Solway coast in a desperate attempt to improve his health by sea-bathing. On this occasion he greeted Maria Riddell, an acquaintance of many years, with the words 'Well, madam, have you any commands for the other world?' His final letter, dated 18 July, was to his father-in-law:

Do, for Heaven's sake, send Mrs Armour here immediately. My wife is hourly expecting to be put to bed. Good God! what a situation for her to be in, poor girl, without a friend! I returned from sea-bathing quarters today, and my medical friends would almost persuade me that I am better; but I think and feel that my strength is so gone that the disorder will prove fatal to me.[35]

Burns died in Dumfries on 21 July. A son was born on 25 July, the day of his funeral.

NOTES

1. *The Letters of Robert Burns*, ed. J. De Lancey Ferguson and G. Ross Roy (Oxford, 1985), I, 134, autobiographical letter to Dr John Moore, 2 August 1787.

2. *The Works of Robert Burns with an Account of his Life*, ed. James Currie (2nd ed., 1801), I, 88.

3. *Letters*, I, 135, to Moore.

4. *Ibid.*, I, 135.

5. Currie, I, 69-70.

6. *Letters*, I, 140-1, to Moore.

7. *Ibid.*, I, 139.

8. Currie, I, 361.

9. David Daiches, *Robert Burns* (1952), pp. 58-9.

10. *Letters*, I, 192, to Richard Brown, 30 December 1787.

11. *Ibid.*, I, 143, to Moore.

12. *Ibid.*, I, 142, to Moore.

13. *Ibid.*, I, 143, to Moore.

14. *Ibid.*, I, 143, to Moore.

15. See *Robert Burns's Commonplace Book 1783-5*, ed. J. C. Ewing and Davidson Cook [Glasgow, 1938], with introduction by David Daiches, 1965.

16. *Letters*, I, 143-4, to Moore.

17. *Ibid.*, I, 143, to Moore.

18. *Ibid.*, I, 145, to Moore.

19. Anderson to James Currie, 28 September 1799, *Burns Chronicle* (1925), xxxiv, p. 12.

20. Mackenzie's review is reproduced in *Robert Burns: The Critical Heritage*, ed. D. A. Low (1974), pp. 67-71.

21. *Letters*, I, 70, to Gavin Hamilton, 7 December 1786.

22. Anderson to Currie, 28 September 1799, *Burns Chronicle* (1925), xxxiv, p. 14.

23. J. G. Lockhart, *Life of Burns*, 1828; text here from *Burns: The Critical Heritage*, p. 261-2.

24. *Letters*, I, 145, to Moore.

25. F. B. Snyder, *The Life of Robert Burns* (New York, 1932), p. 252.

26. *Robert Burns's Commonplace Book 1783-85* ed. J. C. Ewing and D. Cook (1965 ed.), p. 38.

27. *Letters*, I, 101, 22 March 1787, to Mrs Dunlop.

28. *Robert Burns's Tour of the Borders 5 May-1 June 1787* ed. Raymond Lamont Brown (1972), p. 24.

29. *Ibid.*, p. 27.

30. *Notes On Scottish Song by Robert Burns* ed. James C. Dick (1908), p. 33.

31. F. B. Snyder, *The Life of Robert Burns*, p. 274.

32. *Letters*, I, 247, 2 March 1788, to Mrs M'Lehose.

33. *Letters*, II, 381, c. 1 June 1796, to James Johnson.

34. Manuscript diary of James MacDonald, St Andrews University Library: cf. D. A. Low, 'A last supper with Scotland's bard', *The Scotsman*, 22 January 1983.

35. *Letters*, II, 391, 18 July 1796, to James Armour.

CHAPTER 2

VALUES, VOICE and VERSE FORM

What were Burns's motives for writing poetry? Like many other poets before and since, he offered conflicting explanations at different points in his life. These reflect his changing moods, and particular contexts, in conversation, letters, and print. It is clear that above all, he rhymed for his own pleasure, just as — apparently without ever winning much praise for it — he enjoyed playing the fiddle. He began with a lovesong, and from his teens had the habit of making verses to impress girls and express 'the softer passions'. By his mid twenties he was keenly interested in making a mark as one of the poets of his own district of Ayrshire. The matter might have rested there, save for the strong ambition natural in any young poet of outstanding ability. By the time he decided to bring out *Poems, Chiefly in The Scottish Dialect* at Kilmarnock in 1786, Burns had hopes that, even if he should not be lucky enough to attract notice, he might be worthy of a place in Scottish poetry as a successor to Ramsay and Fergusson.

The Kilmarnock volume carries a Preface which makes clear that the poet's first aim is to describe the way of life and values of country people like himself.[1] He draws a distinction between his own intimate involvement with his subject and the very different approach of a learned poet amusing himself, 'perhaps amid the elegancies and idlenesses of upper life', by choosing a 'rural theme'. He has been led to sing (or celebrate) 'the sentiments and manners, he felt and saw in himself and his rustic compeers around him, in his and their native language'.

Burns follows this characteristically truthful claim with an equally revealing explanation of his reasons for writing. 'To amuse himself with the little creations of his own fancy, amid the toils and fatigues of a laborious life; to transcribe the various feelings, the loves, the griefs, the hopes, the fears, in his own breast; to find some kind of counterpoise to the struggles of a world, always an alien scene, a task uncouth to the poetical mind; these were his motives for courting the Muses, and in these he found Poetry to be its own reward'.

Perhaps the most striking phrase in this sentence is 'to find some kind of counterpoise . . .' Life was dauntingly hard for Burns and those fated like himself to wear the 'russet coat' of the working tenant farmer. In his case it was made all the more frustrating because he knew himself to have exceptional abilities, and yet was denied any real prospect of bettering himself. His letters and early poetry both show that he felt acutely the injustice of an economic and social system which offered scant opportunity to anyone born without capital. In itself, the writing of poetry might not succeed in bringing about a change either in his personal circumstances or in the distribution of wealth. It was, nevertheless, a congenial form of activity in its own right and one with much more purpose to it than mere dreaming. Through writing, Burns found a forward momentum and outlet for his ideas to set against the daily drudgery of working on the land — hence his comment on 'some kind of counterpoise'.

Writing can be a form of therapy for the one who writes. In this same part of the Preface to the Kilmarnock *Poems* Burns explains that one of his reasons for writing poetry has been a need for self-expression — 'to transcribe the various feelings, the loves, the griefs, the hopes, the fears in his own breast'. These words, with their emphasis on the authentic rendering of feeling, might almost be taken as the declaration of faith of any Romantic poet of the next generation. And indeed there is

a sense in which even at the outset of his career, Burns
was committed to emotional self-affirmation in poetry to a
degree which was very unusual at this date. A song such
as 'Corn Rigs', for example, is in no sense merely a
'literary' exercise, but instead a direct and intimate
communication from the heart.

It was upon a Lammas night,
  When corn rigs are bonie,   *ridges*
Beneath the moon's unclouded light,
  I held awa to Annie:
The time flew by, wi' tentless head,   *careless*
  Till 'tween the late and early;
Wi' sma' persuasion she agreed,   *little*
  To see me thro' the barley. . . .

The sky was blue, the wind was still,
  The moon was shining clearly;
I set her down, wi' right good will,
  Amang the rigs o' barley:
I ken't her heart was a' my ain;
  I lov'd her most sincerely;
I kiss'd her owre and owre again,   *over*
  Amang the rigs o' barley.

I lock'd her in my fond embrace;
  Her heart was beating rarely:
My blessings on that happy place,
  Amang the rigs o' barley!
But by the moon and stars so bright,
  That shone that night so clearly!
She ay shall bless that happy night,
  Amang the rigs o' barley.

I hae been blythe wi' Comrades dear;
  I hae been merry drinking;
I hae been joyfu' gath'rin gear;
  I hae been happy thinking:

But a' the pleasures e'er I saw,
　　Tho' three times doubl'd fairly,
That happy night was worth them a',
　　Amang the rigs o' barley.

CHORUS

Corn rigs, an' barley rigs,
　　An' corn rigs are bonie:
I'll ne'er forget that happy night,
　　Amang the rigs wi' Annie.

In this song Burns achieves with apparent ease what
Keats was to describe as 'the true voice of feeling'.
Remodelling a rather insipid and coy love-song of Allan
Ramsay, and keeping in mind the fine folk-melody to
which it is set, the poet here is directly and uninhibitedly
personal. His song succeeds — even without the presence
of the tune, but to a much greater degree when set to it —
in capturing the ringing pride and delight of a real
individual who has been lucky in love. Although its art
conceals art, it lives up to Burns's claim in his Preface
about his motives for writing by being a 'transcript' of
joy, pure and simple.

　　Burns's voice as a poet is distinctively personal
throughout the Kilmarnock *Poems*. Time and again we
hear what seem to be the accents of felt experience. His
moods naturally vary. He may be at a high point of
happiness, as in 'Corn Rigs'. Or, quite differently, he
may be fatigued at the end of the day and in need of fresh
inspiration, as in the opening of 'The Vision':

flail	The Thresher's weary *flingin-tree*,
whole	The lee-lang day had tir'd me;
closed eye	And when the Day had clo'd his e'e,
	Far i' the West,
inner room	Ben i' the *Spence*, right pensivelie,
went	I gaed to rest.

There, lanely, by the ingle-cheek,   lonely   fire-side
I sat and ey'd the spewing reek,   smoke
That fill'd, wi' hoast-provoking smeek,   cough- smoke
    The auld, clay biggin;   old   building
And heard the restless rattons squeak   rats
    About the riggin.   roof

All in this mottie, misty clime,   dusty
I backward mus'd on wasted time,
How I had spent my *youthfu' prime,*
    An' done nae-thing,   nothing
But stringing blethers up in rhyme   idle talk
    For fools to sing.

Had I to guid advice but harket,   listened
I might, by this, hae led a market,   have
Or strutted in a Bank and clarket   written up
    My *Cash-Account;*
While here, half-made, half-fed, half-
    sarket,   -shirted
    Is a' th' amount.   all

The mood may change, but the poet's communicative
candour does not. Burns's wry humour in this passage is
no less one of his characteristic ways of responding to
experience than the carefree swagger of 'Corn Riggs'. As
it develops, 'The Vision' faithfully enacts the belief about
poetry as 'counterpoise' set out in the Preface, demon-
strating the process of having personal horizons widened
which a committed poet may expect to be able to set
against life's round of wearying tasks. Coila, who visits
the poet, shows him that poetry is indeed 'its own
reward'.

    The most immediately noticeable feature of the descrip-
tion which opens 'The Vision' is its sheer realism. The
cottage and smoky fireside are there before our eyes. As
well as having a remarkable gift for communicating

feeling, Burns is skilled at creating a sense of the physical
world about him. His curiosity extends in every direction,
with human life at the centre of the scene. This balance of
interests is characteristic. The first and most important
strength of the Kilmarnock collection, in fact, is the poet's
clear-sighted observation — of himself, of others, and of
the surrounding environment. He has followed the
precept 'look in your heart and write', but without losing
touch with external reality.

In his devotion to accurate recording of what he sees, as
well as of what he feels, Burns remains true to the values
of the eighteenth century. His stress on emotion,
especially in song, anticipates Romantic literary practice,
but his outlook has been strongly influenced by the
bracing combined effect of the realities of country living
and of neoclassical ideas of the mimetic function of art, as
practised for example by Alexander Pope, whose poetry
he admired. In all this, he belongs to mainstream
eighteenth-century tradition.

Coila refers in 'The Vision' to Burns's
'manners-painting strains'. This phrase connects with a
comment in the Preface to the Kilmarnock poems which
has already been cited: 'he sings the sentiments and
manners, he felt and saw in himself and his rustic
compeers around him, in his and their native language'.
By 'manners-painting' Burns means the genial rendering
of the way of life and values by which members of a social
group (or groups) live. The emphasis on Scots is signifi-
cant here; Burns has chosen to use the vernacular in
certain poems both because he is at home in it and
because he knows it to belong in an integral way to his
subject. Examples of poems which describe 'manners' in
this sense in the 1786 collection include 'The Twa Dogs',
'The Holy Fair', 'Halloween', and 'The Cotter's
Saturday Night'. In each of these, while varying his
poetic style and approach according to the topic, Burns
follows the tradition of *genre* painting on the one hand and

of Robert Fergusson's poetry on the other by illustrating facets of the human comedy.

'The Twa Dogs', which opens the book, admirably represents his art in that it expresses with considerable force and subtlety what may be called an incremental social meaning, by means of Scots dialogue and narrative. The poet's main purpose here is to communicate certain home truths about the yawning gulf in outlook and values between the life of rich and poor in rural Ayrshire. Burns deftly accomplishes this by making use of two dogs, who become his *personae* or characters in simulated debate. 'The Twa Dogs' belongs to a long Scottish tradition of animal poems. Like his fifteenth-century predecessor Henryson in such Fables as 'The Uponlandis Mous and the Burges Mous', Burns creates a special satirical effect by having animals talk. Caesar is a Newfoundland belonging to a rich estate-owner. Commendably free himself from any snobbish or exclusive spirit ('the fient a pride na pride had he'), he discloses to his companion the shortcomings of the wealthy — including snobbish pride — all of which he has seen at firsthand. In conversation with him is Luath, a poor ploughman's collie, named after an actual dog of the poet's. His role in the poem is to register shock at what he learns from Caesar, and to draw attention by contrast to positive qualities in the lives of the long-suffering poor, as for instance in this passage:

> They're no sae wretched's ane wad
>   think;   *so   as one would*
> Tho' constantly on poortith's brink,   *poverty's*
> They're sae accustom'd wi' the sight,
> The view o't gies them little fright.   *gives*
>
> Then chance and fortune are sae
>   guided,
> They're ay in less or mair provided;   *more*
> An' tho' fatigu'd wi' close employment,
> A blink o' rest's a sweet enjoyment.

> The dearest comfort o' their lives,
> Their grushie weans an' faithfu' wives;
> The *prattling things* are just their pride,
> That sweetens a' their fire side.

thriving children

Here and throughout, we see the representatives of Luath's class in a good light. To use a phrase Burns was to apply to himself in a song, they are 'contented wi' little, and canty [happy] wi' mair'. Clearly, the poet has selected the details he chooses to present with care, so as to emphasise certain social values. What makes the words of the dogs seem exceptionally persuasive is that they carry the accent of lived experience; and part of the evidence for this impression is that the diction and speech rhythms of the poem approximate closely to those current even today in Lowland Scotland. For example, in the lines

> Then chance and fortune are sae
>   guided,
> They're ay in less or mair provided

the poet combines predominantly English vocabulary with Scots pronunciation in a maner which closely matches colloquial usage. (As it happens, the Scots forms *sae, ay,* and *mair*, can still be heard every day; 'ay less or mair' is idiomatic; and this form of sententious, near-proverbial saying — or homespun consolation — is recognisable as a variant of one sort of aphorism found among working people both within and beyond the boundaries of Scotland.) Such an example shows that Burns's ear for the language spoken about him is very sharp. Beyond this, he knows how to make his written words convey in a form which seems authentically that of the people, a democratic point of view and reflections on living and social class which are at once humorous and challenging. What Caesar and Luath have to say in 'The Twa Dogs', and the manner of saying it, are likely to persuade the reader by the end of the poem that he has been privileged to over-hear something very close to the authentic country talk of

Burns's Ayrshire. The poem turns on ideas about what community and human sharing ought to mean and what they actually look like in practice. Point of view is everything, and adroitly handled. Burns's invention of Caesar and Luath and their discursive foray serve his purpose so well that at times it becomes all but impossible to distinguish between the poet and his creation. Potential communal values and the individual voice are then indivisible.

'The Cotter's Saturday Night' differs from 'The Twa Dogs' in that it is predominantly solemn in tone. 'Manners-painting' humour does occur, for instance in the treatment of the mother's pardonable pride in her cheese, but it is secondary and incidental. Another difference between the poems is related to this one. Whereas Scots is employed throughout 'The Twa Dogs', Burns makes use of dignified English diction at certain points in 'The Cotter's Saturday Night'. This is not a sign of any false pretension or cultural betrayal on the poet's part, but instead an accurate reflection of the linguistic habit of Scotland since the Reformation, when the English Bible was first adopted to be used in Scottish pulpits. In its own way, 'The Cotter's Saturday Night' is remarkably true to what had for long been an accepted spoken norm in Scotland, namely the use of Scots as the natural first choice for most secular purposes, and by contrast of English as the language of worship and devotion. Literary tradition had reinforced and accentuated the division before Burns's time. By alternating in 'The Cotter's Saturday Night' between his native Scots and passages of reflection in English the poet simply develops in his own distinctive manner a stylistic variation already present in the literature he inherits from the past.

It is useful in considering 'The Cotter's Saturday Night' to establish this point at the outset, because the fact that Robert Fergusson's 'The Farmer's Ingle' — which Burns knew and admired — is wholly in Scots has on

occasion misled students of Burns into arguing that his
use of English in passages of solemn reflection is in itself
somehow spurious. In fact, the two poets have different
aims in view. Fergusson in 'The Farmer's Ingle' excels in
genre painting *per se*, rendering with satisfyingly exact and
well-chosen Scots phrases a characteristic farmhouse
kitchen interior . . .

well knows housewife	Weel kens the gudewife that the pleughs require
meal	A heartsome meltith, and refreshing
draught	synd
ale blazin	O' nappy liquor, o'er a bleezing fire;
sore poverty cannot	Sair wark and poortith douna weel be join'd.
	Wi' buter'd bannocks now the girdle
steams	reeks,
corner barrel creams	I' the far nook the bowie briskly reams;
broth chimney	The readied kail stand by the chimla cheeks,
roof hot	And had the riggin het wi' welcome steams,
which	Whilk than the daintiest kitchen nicer seems.

Burns, in contrast, wishes to present the high point of the
life of a family, namely their Saturday evening meal and
worship. He builds on the example of Fergusson's poem,
but adds an explicit emotional and religious dimension of
his own, which requires modulation to a poetic style
without precedent in 'The Farmer's Ingle'. Specifically,
he innovates by creating both Jenny's love situation and
five stanzas about the family's act of worship, and invests
much of his picture with overtones of the idealised
'domestic sublime'. The first is presented initially
through lively description:

But hark! a rap comes gently to the door;
   Jenny, wha kens the meaning o' the same,   who knows
Tells how a neebor lad came o'er the   neighbour
    moor,
    To do some errands, and convoy her   escort
     hame.
The wily Mother sees the *conscious flame*
    Sparkle in *Jenny's* e'e, and flush her   eye
     cheek,
With heart-struck, anxious care enquires
    his name,
    While *Jenny* hafflins is afraid to speak;   nearly
Weel-pleas'd the Mother hears, it's nae   well no
    wild, worthless *Rake*.

But then, after adding a stanza about the 'kindly welcome' the youth receives from Jenny, and about how her Mother is

    Weel-pleas'd to think her *bairn's*
     respected like the lave

Burns proceeds to moralise very explicitly in English for two stanzas . . .

O happy love! where love like this is
    found!
    O heart-felt raptures! bliss beyond
     compare!
I've paced much this weary, *mortal round*,
    And sage EXPERIENCE bids me this
     declare —
'If Heaven a draught of heavenly pleasure
    spare,
    'One *cordial* in this melancholy *Vale*,
'Tis when a youthful, loving, *modest* Pair,
    'In other's arms, breathe out the tender
     tale,
'Beneath the milk-white thorn that scents
    the ev'ning gale.'

D

Is there in human form, that bears a
    heart —
  A Wretch! a Villain! lost to love and
    truth!
That can, with studied, sly, ensnaring art,
  Betray sweet Jenny's unsuspecting
    youth?
Curse on his perjur'd arts! dissembling
    smooth!
  Are *Honor, Virtue, Conscience,* all exil'd?
Is there no Pity, no relenting Ruth,
  Points to the Parents fondling o'er their
    Child?
Then paints the *ruin'd Maid,* and *their*
    distraction wild!

One recent critic has described the second of these stanzas
as 'one of the most nauseating ever published by a repu-
table poet . . . hysterical rhodomontade'. It is clear that
there is a temporary breach of poetic tact on Burns's part
— seen not in the use of English as such but in the
strained tone — but such severe criticism as that quoted
seems excessive itself. Interestingly, in Burns's day and
well into the nineteenth century these particular stanzas
were greatly admired. Why? Historically, the truth is that
widespread and popular conventions of explicit moral
sentiment in different forms of art and general discourse
allowed them to be. The voice which Burns adopts in the
first of these stanzas

  I've paced much this weary, *mortal round*

is reminiscent of the stylised response of Harley, the 'man
of feeling' in Henry Mackenzie's novel of that name,
which Burns prized 'next to the Bible'. Burns is contributing here to a continuum of literary sentiment which
also includes the scenes of heroism and pathos Dickens
was to create in his best-selling novels. Taste has simply
changed since.

What is in danger of being missed in 'The Cotter's Saturday Night' in our own day is the depth of Burns's Biblical knowledge and awareness of Scottish Presbyterian tradition. Stanza 13, for instance, provides a description of the family singing 'Scotia's holy lays'. Several of these are named; and historical research confirms that Burns has selected in *Dundee*, *Martyrs*, and *Elgin* three of the melodies which would indeed have been used on such an occasion. There is a no less carefully worked out connection between the family values of the whole poem, clearly identifiable Old and New Testament texts which are cited by the poet, and the nature of the parents' prayer when they are alone

> That HE who stills the *raven's* clam'rous
> nest,
> And decks the *lily* fair in flow'ry pride,
> Would, in the way *His Wisdom* sees the
> best,
> For *them* and for their *little ones* provide;
> But chiefly, in their hearts with *Grace*
> *divine* preside.

'The Cotter's Saturday Night' is fervently patriotic as well as moral, and this feature too has drawn adverse comment in the twentieth century. In fact, Burns's idealised treatment in the poem of love, family, and nation, and especially the coda 'From scenes like these, old SCOTIA's grandeur springs . . .' have provoked a modern Ayrshireman, Gordon Williams, to write an entire novel in angry disagreement. The last three stanzas of the poem are quoted in full at the beginning of *From Scenes Like These* (1968), which presents a very different picture of broken relationships in the urban industrial wasteland. It is possible, however, to admire the narrative energy of Williams' novel without feeling any necessity to agree with his rejection of a good poem in which Burns, remembering his father's example, happens to have

chosen to celebrate without irony a number of the positive
social and spiritual values of Christian civilisation. Moreover, it is surely evidence of a powerful current of life in
'The Cotter's Saturday Night' that after two hundred
years its values and poetic style can elicit a personal
response.

The same is certainly true of one of the most celebrated
of Burns's animal poems, 'To a Mouse, on turning her
up in her Nest, with the Plough, November 1785'. What
stands out in this poem is a wryly aware tenderness
towards a vulnerable fellow-creature. Once again, and
unexpectedly, there is underpinning from Burns's
knowledge of the Bible. Stanza three draws both on
Burns's superb command of spoken Scots and on his
memory of a religious text:

not at times	I doubt na, whyles, but thou may *thieve;*
must	What then? poor beastie, thou maun live!
occasional ear sheaf	A *daimen-icker* in a *thrave*
small	'S a sma' request:
rest	I'll get a blessing wi' the lave,
	An' never miss't!

Here the expression 'a daimen-icker', which the Scottish
National Dictionary classifies as a specifically Ayrshire
usage, means an occasional ear; a 'thrave' is a measure
equivalent to two stooks of corn, or twenty-four sheaves.
Burns's point is that what the mouse needs in order to
survive will never be missed. This much results from a
farmer's practical common-sense observation. But in the
last two lines of the stanza, Burns strengthens his resolve,
and places it in a long perspective, by recalling an injunc-
tion in the Book of Deuteronomy:[3]

> When thou cuttest down thine harvest in thy field,
> and hast forgot a sheaf in the field, thou shalt not go
> again to fetch it: it shall be for the stranger, for the
> fatherless, and for the widow: that the Lord thy God
> may bless thee in all the work of thine hands.

In the stanza immediately preceding this, Burns has
described the mouse as his 'fellow-mortal', apologising for
the rude way in which Man has broken 'Nature's social
union'. To this general philosophical position, a familiar
one in eighteenth-century thought, he now adds Old
Testament example. The harvest-mouse from this point
of view becomes 'the stranger', towards whom charity is a
solemn duty.

'To a Mouse' gains its effects mainly through the poet's
relaxed tone; it is as if we were privileged to be with the
poet as he muses to himself in the field at the time of the
incident. An echo of the command 'thou shalt not go
again . . . it shall be for the stranger' is no more than a
thought in the passing — yet one which subtly adds to the
meaning of what is being said. The glancing way in which
it is introduced can be compared with a similar example
of Burns's poised handling of ideas in 'The Twa Dogs',
this time for a comic purpose. We are informed, and it is
deliberately in the passing, that *Luath* is a name with
certain associations. The ploughman

in his freaks had *Luath* ca'd him;	called
After some dog in **Highlan Sang*,	Highland Song
Was made lang syne, lord knows how lang.	long ago

Burns adds a footnote identifying the literary beast in
question as 'Cuchullin's dog in Ossian's Fingal'. His
throwaway last line, which is likely to be read quite
casually, conceals a brilliantly apt comment on the
controversy raging in Burns's day over the allegedly
authentic fragments of ancient Gaelic poetry which had
been published by James Macpherson. Whether in reflec-
tive or witty mood, Burns wears his learning lightly.

In its final stanzas, 'To a Mouse' contains another
example of hidden allusion and exploits a borrowed idea.
The source in this instance is an eighteenth-century
English text, Dr Johnson's philosophical fable *Rasselas*.

Burns writes:

alone	But Mousie, thou art no thy-lane,
	In proving *foresight* may be vain:
	The best laid schemes o' *Mice* an' *Men,*
often go astray	Gang aft agley,
leave	An lea'e us nought but grief an' pain,
	For promis'd joy!

Still, thou art blest, compar'd wi' *me*!
The *present* only toucheth thee:
eye   But Och! I *backward* cast my e'e
     On prospects drear!
cannot   An *forward*, tho' I canna *see*,
     I *guess* an' fear!

In these often quoted verses, Burns is recalling a passage from chapter II of Johnson's novel, which presents one of the early insights of Rasselas, the future philosopher prince. 'As he passed through the fields, and saw the animals around him, ''Ye'', said he, ''are happy, and need not envy me that walk thus among you, burdened with myself; nor do I, ye gentle beings, envy your felicity, for it is not the felicity of man. I have many distresses from which ye are free: I fear pain when I do not feel it; I sometimes shrink at evils recollected, and sometimes start at evils anticipated: surely the equity of Providence has balanced peculiar sufferings with peculiar enjoyments'.

Johnson's prose influences the conclusion Burns reaches, but hardly his style. The natural manner in which the poet addresses the mouse is easily the most distinctive feature of the poem. In part, this flows from natural ability and genuine feeling on the poet's part; and in part from the fact that Burns is using a particularly congenial verse form. It should be stated that even as early as 1786 he is a versatile metrist, with different forms at his command. 'To A Mouse' is one of many poems in the Kilmarnock edition written in a metre known as 'Standart Habbie'.

The form derives its name from a poem by the seventeenth-century Scots vernacular poet Robert Sempill of Beltrees. 'The Life and Death of Habbie Simson, the Piper of Kilbarchan' is a comic elegy, a form which can be compared in spirit to playing at a jazz funeral. It pays tribute, but not too solemnly. Thus we are informed that at weddings Habbie had the habit of mischievously appearing behind people's backs . . .

And then, beside his valiant acts,	
At bridals he wan many placks;	coins
He bobbit ay behind folk's backs	always bobbed
And shook his head.	
Now we want many merry cracks	jokes
Sen Habbie's dead.[4]	since

Sempill's six-line stanza greatly appealed to Allan Ramsay, who employed it for a new communicative purpose in an exchange of verse-epistles with William Hamilton of Gilbertfield. Other of Ramsay's poems in Sempill's measure come under the heading of mock elegy — and this remained the main application of 'Standart Habbie' in Fergusson's hands also. Fergusson, however, further widened the range to include social satire in poems such as 'Braid Claith' and 'The Rising of the Session'.

It is difficult to overestimate the significance of 'Standart Habbie' in the case of Burns. He liked the form from the beginning, and practised with it so often that skill in its use has became instinctive. Byron's liberating discovery in Italy in 1816 of *ottava rima*, which made possible the writing of such satires as *Beppo* and *The Vision of Judgement*, is in a sense comparable. Both poets were enabled through the use of a particular verse form to write in a relaxed colloquial style, with a resulting gain in persuasiveness. But there is one crucial difference, in that Burns found a metre which suited him early in his career as a poet, and used 'Standart Habbie' for more than satire alone. He experimented and greatly extended the range of its possible applications both in the Kilmarnock *Poems* and subsequently.

'The Death and Dying Words of Poor Mailie', written in rhyming couplets, is Burns's earliest sustained poem in Lowland Scots. 'Standart Habbie' is used for the traditional purpose of mock elegy in an accompanying piece, 'Mailie's Elegy', written much later when Burns was already planning to publish his work. This is very much in the style of Hamilton of Gilbertfield's 'Last Dying Words of Bonny Heck, a Famous Grey-Hound in the Shire of Fife'. For example, in the first stanza Burns marks the short fourth and sixth lines by making use of a rhyme, 'remead' with 'dead', which had become traditional in this sort of poem — we find it in 'Bonny Heck', in Ramsay's 'Elegy on Maggy Johnston', and in Fergusson's 'Elegy, on the Death of Mr David Gregory, late Professor of Mathematics in the University of St Andrews'. Burns is mourning the loss of his ewe, and he set about the task with vigour:

	Lament in rhyme, lament in prose,
salt	Wi' saut tears trickling down your nose;
poet's	Our *Bardie's* fate is at a close,
all hope of remedy	Past a' remead!
cope-stone	The last, sad cape-stane of his woes;
	Poor Mailie's dead!

The approach here follows the expected pattern of irony and humorous compliment ('She was nae get o' moorlan tips/Wi' tauted ket, an' hairy hips'). The first three lines of each stanza illustrate an aspect of the theme, and then inbuilt rhythmical variation helps to give comic emphasis. After ringing the changes on the theme of Mailie's merits, Burns brings the poem to a self-mocking climax:

O, a' ye *Bards* on bonie DOON!   all
An' wha on AIRE your chanters tune!
Come, join the melancholious croon
   O' *Robin's* reed!
His heart will never get aboon!   above
   His *Mailie's* dead!

Burns was subsequently to make use of 'Standart Habbie'
in mock elegy with an identifiable person, Tam Samson,
as his subject. Here a comic twist comes at the end of the
poem with the disclosure that Tam is not dead after all but
very much alive. Technically more innovative than 'Tam
Samson's Elegy' is a poem dating from 1788, his 'Elegy
on Capt M____ H____, A Gentleman who held the
Patent for his Honours immediately from Almighty
God!'. Matthew Henderson had been a valued neighbour
of the poet's when he lived in St James's Square in Edinburgh during the previous winter. In his 'Elegy', Burns
succeeds in making the six-line stanza a suitable form for
the expression of genuine grief.

He's gane! he's gane! he's frae us torn,   gone   from
The ae best fellow e'er was born!   one
Thee, Matthew, Nature's sel shall mourn   self
   By wood and wild,
Where, haply, Pity strays forlorn,
   Frae man exil'd.

In particular, Henderson having been a lover of the out-
doors, he includes a nature sequence which is one of the
loveliest and most resonant in Scottish poetry. Only part
of this can be quoted here; but the sequence as a whole
vividly illustrates Burns's skill in exploiting the
vernacular strength of the Habbie Simson tradition while
treating the form with a new seriousness in the manner of
classical pastoral elegy:

near neighbours stars	Ye hills, neer neebors o' the starns,
	That proudly cock your cresting cairns;
eagles	Ye cliffs, the haunts of sailing yearns,
	Where Echo slumbers:
children	Come join, ye Nature's sturdiest bairns,
	My wailing numbers.
wood-pigeon knows	Mourn, ilka grove the cushat kens;
small woods of hazel	Ye hazly shaws and briery dens;
little streams meandering	Ye burnies, wimpling down your glens,
	Wi' toddlin din,
strong bounds	Or foaming, strang, wi' hasty stens,
from waterfall	Frae lin to lin. . . .
	Mourn, ye wee songsters o' the wood;
grouse crop	Ye grouss that crap the heather bud;
cloud	Ye curlews calling thro' a clud;
	Ye whistling plover;
partridge	And mourn, ye whirring paitrick brood;
gone	He's gane for ever!
	Mourn, sooty coots, and speckled teals;
	Ye fisher herons, watching eels;
	Ye duck and drake, wi' airy wheels
	Circling the lake;
	Ye bitterns, till the quagmire reels,
roar	Rair for his sake.
corn-crakes	Mourn, clamouring craiks at close o' day,
clover	'Mang fields o' flowering claver gay;
	And when ye wing your annual way
cold	Frae our cauld shore,
who	Tell thae far warlds, wha lie in clay,
whom	Wham we deplore.

Within the Kilmarnock collection, 'The Vision' exempli-
fies another way in which Burns widens the range of

'Standart Habbie' to include the communication of
serious ideas. It could be argued that its use in this poem
is symbolic. Burns, after all, is writing in 'The Vision'
about his own aspirations in poetry; it is appropriate that
he should employ his favourite metre. The poem ends
with Coila, his Muse, imparting her most precious
advice:

> To give my counsels all in one,
> Thy *tuneful flame* still careful fan;
> Preserve *the dignity of Man*,
>   With Soul erect;
> And trust, the UNIVERSAL PLAN
>   Will all protect.

> '*And wear thou this*' — She solemn said,
> And bound the *Holly* round my head:
> The polish'd leaves, and berries red,
>   Did rustling play;
> And, like a passing thought, she fled,
>   In light away.

What characterises Burns's handling of the six-line stanza
above all is the aptitude he displays for catching the
rhythms and tones of a speaking voice. It is no accident
that his 'Address to the Deil' is in 'Standart Habbie'; nor
that he should choose the metre for a virtuoso display of
spoken Scots, 'The auld Farmer's new-year-morning
Salutation to his auld Mare, Maggie, on giving her the
accustomed ripp of Corn to hansel in the new year'.
Intimacy and frankness characterise both.

    There are no fewer than seven verse-epistles in the
Kilmarnock edition, and all but two are in 'Standart
Habbie'. A frequently reprinted verse-epistle exchange
between Allan Ramsay and William Hamilton was the
main example which Burns had in mind when he sent to
men of his area like John Lapraik (a stranger) and David
Sillar (an old friend) a series of 'letters' in verse

expressing his hopes and anxieties and commenting on some of life's problems and rewards. Burns encouraged the recipients to reply in kind. Although his wish to belong to an active group of mid-Ayrshire poets remained to some extent unfulfilled, it is of interest that both Lapraik and Sillar were stimulated by his success to publish books of poems of their own. For his part, Burns clearly felt the need of stimulus and support from friends who shared his interests, and nursed an ambition to see his native county win recognition as one of those in Scotland noted for the writing of poetry. Thus we find him writing to William Simpson of Ochiltree, in May 1785:

> *Ramsay* an' famous *Ferguson*
> Gied *Forth* an' *Tay* a lift aboon;
> *Yarrow* an' *Tweed,* to monie a tune,
>   Owre Scotland rings,
> While *Irwin, Lugar, Aire* an' *Doon,*
>   Naebody sings.

(glosses: gave above — Gied ... aboon; many — Yarrow; over — Owre; nobody — Naebody)

> Th'*Illisus, Tiber Thames* an' *Seine,*
> Glide sweet in monie a tunefu' line;
> But *Willie* set your fit to mine,
>   An' cock your crest,
> We'll gar our streams an' burnies shine
>   Up wi' the best.

(glosses: foot — fit; make streams — gar our streams)

> We'll sing auld COILA'S plains and fells,
> Her moors red-brown wi' heather bells,
> Her banks an' braes, her dens an' dells,
>   Where glorious WALLACE
> Aft bure the gree, as story tells,
>   Frae Suthron billies.

(glosses: hillsides — braes; often won supremacy — Aft bure the gree; from English fellows — Frae Suthron billies)

Revealingly, this particular passage leads on to a meditation on the beauty of Nature. According to Burns, no poet is truly worthy of the name until he has learned to wander by himself along a country stream, musing on nothing more material than 'heart-felt sang'. Then, by one of the swift transitions which his expertise in the literary form allows, Burns sets up an opposition between lovers of the open air of this type and mere worldly persons:

The warly race may drudge an' drive,	worldly
Hog-shouther, jundie, stretch an' strive,	jostle, elbow
Let me fair NATURE'S face descrive,	
And I, wi' Pleasure,	
Shall let the busy, grumbling hive	
Bum owre their treasure.	

As a group, the verse-epistles are characterised by exceptional flexibility of style, and by their being repeatedly used to enable Burns to share with a like-minded friend his personal values, and perhaps to come to terms with a social challenge. That this process continues when the poet chooses a different metre can be seen from his 'Epistle to Davie, A Brother Poet', in which he handles the complex and difficult mediaeval stanza associated with Alexander Montgomerie's poem 'The Cherrie and the Slae'. The need for internal rhyme in the 'wheel' with which each 14-line stanza concludes is demanding; but what lends the poem distinction is Burns's determination to make the best of his lot, come what may.

It's hardly in a body's pow'r,	a person's
To keep, at times, frae being sour,	from
To see how things are shar'd;	
But *best o' chiels* are whyles in want,	best of fellows sometimes
While *Coofs* on countless thousands rant,	fools
And ken na how to wair't:	know not spend
But DAVIE lad, ne'er fash your head,	trouble
Tho' we hae little gear,	property
We're fit to win our daily bread,	
As lang's we're hale and fier:	long sound

ask no more	'Mair spier na, nor fear na',
old fig	Auld age ne'er mind a feg;
worst	The last o't, the warst o't,
	Is only but to beg.

Throughout his career as a poet and song-writer Burns wrote most fluently when he had a particular and immediate stimulus, in the wish to please a friend or lover, to match a tune, or to get something off his chest. In that sense, his art is best understood in social terms, as a form of direct communication from person to person. With all allowance made for self-deprecating irony, he is in truth no merely bookish poetic practitioner seeking to climb Parnassus 'by dint o' Greek', but instead 'a rhymer like by chance', someone engaging in a communicative activity which aims to create pleasure. One poem which illustrates his flair for projecting a view of himself calculated to meet with a welcome from his friends is 'On A Scotch Bard Gone To The West Indies'. He wrote this when it looked as though his days in Scotland were numbered. A letter of April 1786 to his friend John Kennedy sketches part of the background, 'Already the holy beagles, the houghmagandie pack [fornication pack, i.e. the kirk session], begin to snuff the scent, & I expect every moment to see them cast off, & hear them after me in full cry [because of Jean Armour's pregnancy]: but as I am an old fox, I shall give them dodging and doubling for it; & by & bye, I intend to earth among the mountains of Jamaica'. Exactly how serious Burns became about emigrating in the months ahead is open to debate; but he went so far as to book his passage, and the evidence suggests that it was largely the chance success of his *Poems* which, in combination with 'the feelings of a father', prevented him from leaving by the autumn.

Because it is written in 'Standart Habbie', 'On A Scotch Bard Gone to the West Indies', is not accompanied by a tune. It is, however, a poem which has linguistic features associated with song, as well as with vigorous speech. Burns's diction, which is charged with rhythmical energy, is that of social intimacy, rather than of formal writing. He opens by addressing congenial male companions, fellow-rhymers among them:

A' ye wha live by sowps of drink,	all you mouthfuls
A' ye who live by crambo-clink,	doggerel verse
A' ye wha live and never think,	
Come, mourn wi' me!	
Our *billie's* gien us a' a jink,	fellow slipped past us all
An' owre the Sea.	over

Lament him a' ye rantan core,	riotous merry company
Wha dearly like a random-splore;	careless frolic
Nae mair he'll join the *merry roar,*	no more
In social key;	
For now he's taen anither shore,	taken another
An' owre the Sea!	

The poet then identifies members of the other sex to whom he looks for especially sympathetic interest in his welfare . . .

The bonie lasses weel may wiss him,	well wish
And in their dear *petitions* place him,	
The widows, wives, an' a' may bless him,	
Wi' tearfu'e'e;	eye
For weel I wat they'll fairly miss him	
That's owre the Sea!	

O Fortune, they hae room to grumble!	
Hadst thou taen aff some drowsy	
bummle,	impotent bungler
What can do nought but fyke an' fumble,	fidget
'Thad been nae plea;	it would have no
But he was gleg as onie wumble,	lively gimlet
That's owre the sea!	

After this, the poem presents in narrative outline the circumstances which have led Burns to think of emigrating to Jamaica. There is a reference to gathering Misfortune suddenly unleashing a bitter blast; then, although he does not name her, Burns alludes unmistakably to Jean Armour:

giddy wench broke

> A Jillet brak his heart at last,
>   Ill may she be!
> So, took a birth afore the mast,
>   An' owre the sea.

Not even so compellingly personal a motive for emigration as this is allowed to destroy the cheerful mood of the poem, however. It is typical of Burns that at a point in 'On A Scotch Bard' where he is dealing with particularly sensitive autobiographical material he should contrive to lighten the tone and divert attention from just how badly hurt he feels by creating a rhyming series to match 'cummock' (a short staff). 'Stomach' is obvious; but he shows ingenuity by introducing 'drummock', a Scots word which he glosses as 'meal and water mixed raw'. (Part of the pleasure to be derived from writing, hearing, or reading relaxed social poetry relates to unexpected or difficult rhymes. Their use for purposes of incidental amusement is one of several neglected affinities between Burns and Byron as verse satirists.) Here, without making it too obvious, he is touching on the fundamental reasons for his planned emigration:

staff

oatmeal and cold water

wrapped buttocks

> To tremble under Fortune's cummock,
> On scarce a bellyfu' o' *drummock*,
> Wi' his proud, independant stomach,
>   Could ill agree;
> So, row't his hurdies in a *hammock*,
>   An' owre the Sea.

'On A Scotch Bard' next shows the poet asking 'Jamaica bodies' to give him 'a cozie biel', and wishing himself well

in a distant land. Interestingly, the poem gives no hint
that Burns may yet be saved from a fate which will entail
exile from Scotland. At the time of writing, presumably
he had no serious thought of staying. In any case, he
cannot have wanted to run the risk of undercutting the
effect created by the rest of the poem:

> Farewell, my *rhyme-composing billie*!
> Your native soil was right ill-willie;   ungenerous
> But may ye flourish like a lily,
>   Now bonilie!
> I'll toast you in my hindmost gillie,   little measure
>   That's owre the Sea!

'On A Scotch Bard' is thus at once personal and public,
light-hearted and a considered statement. Written to
commemorate an event which did not in the end take
place, it shows a defiant yet carefree spirit which Scotland
would inevitably have lost with Burns's departure
overseas.

NOTES

1. Burns's Preface may be read in volume 3 of *The Poems and Songs of Robert Burns* ed. James Kinsley (Oxford, 1968), pp. 971-2, or in *The Kilmarnock Poems* ed. D. A. Low (1985), pp. 175-6.
2. 'The Farmer's Ingle', 11s. 19-27, *Poems by Allan Ramsay and Robert Fergusson* ed. A. M. Kinghorn and A. Law (1974), p. 162.
3. *Deuteronomy* 24.19.
4. 'The Life and Death of Habbie Simson, the piper of Kilbarchan', 11. 49-55, *The Oxford Book of Scottish Verse* ed. John MacQueen and Tom Scott (1966), pp. 306-7.

E

CHAPTER 3

SATIRE

A number of people who knew Burns well noted down their impressions of his character and personality. On this evidence, he was clearly an exceptionally lively, witty conversationalist, whose instinctive responses to anything amusing included a turn for satire. His friend David Sillar, for example, had this to say about Burns as he was in 1781, several years before he began seriously to write poetry:

> Mr Robert Burns was some time in the parish of Tarbolton prior to my acquaintance with him. His social disposition easily procured him acquaintance; but a certain satirical seasoning, with which he and all poetical geniuses are in some degree influenced, while it set the rustic circle in a roar, was not unaccompanied by its kindred attendant, suspicious fear. I recollect hearing his neighbours observe that he had a great deal to say for himself, and that they suspected his principles.[1]

Having observed the poet during his two winters in Edinburgh, the cautious and genteel Henry Mackenzie rather disapproved of Burns's evident lack of respect for some of those he met:

> He indulged his sarcastic humour in talking of men, particularly if he thought them proud, or disdainful of Persons of inferior rank; his Observations were always acute and forcibly expressed. I was walking with him one day, when we met a common Acquaint-

ance not remarkable for Ability or intellectual Endowments. I observed how extremely fat he had lately grown. 'Yes', said Burns, 'and when you have told that you have exhausted the subject of Mr —— Fatness is the only quality you can ascribe to him'.[2]

More expansive on this particular subject than either Sillar or Mackenzie is Maria Riddell (1772-1808), a clever and flirtatious woman who knew Burns in his later years at Dumfries. Shortly after his death, she drafted an essay for a local newspaper giving her assessment of the poet, whose memory she cherished, even although at one time a serious family quarrel had come between Burns and herself. Part of 'Candidior's' character sketch in the *Dumfries Journal* relates directly to Burns's 'dangerous' turn of phrase:

> The keenness of satire was, I am almost at a loss whether to say his forte or his foible; for though nature had endowed him with a portion of the most pointed excellence in that dangerous talent, he suffered it too often to be the vehicle of personal, and sometimes unfounded, animosities. It was not always that sportiveness of humour, that 'unwary pleasantry', which *Sterne* has depictured with touches so conciliatory, but the parts of ridicule were frequently directed as the caprice of the instant suggested, or as the altercations of parties and of persons happened to kindle the restlessness of his spirit into interest or aversion . . . ''Twas no extravagant arithmetic' to say of him, as was said of Yorick, 'that for every ten jokes he got an hundred enemies'; but much allowance will be made by a candid mind for the splenetic warmth of a spirit whom 'distress had spited with the world', and which, unbounded in its intellectual sallies and pursuits, continually experienced the curbs imposed by the waywardness of his fortune . . . It is said that

the celebrated Dr. Johnson professed to 'love a good hater', a temperament that would have singularly adapted him to cherish a prepossession in favor of our bard, who perhaps fell but little short even of the surly Doctor in this qualification, as long as the disposition to ill-will continued; but the warmth of his passions was fortunately corrected by their versatility. He was seldom, indeed never implacable in his resentments. . .[3]

Burns took his 'splenetic warmth' principally from his father, whom he once described as 'the sport of strong passions'. Reinforcing the tendency on the part of her first-born, his red-headed mother, too, had moments when her temper suddenly flared up, but in her case storms would usually blow over quickly and give place to Agnes Burnes's more usual equable and cheerful air. It is easy to imagine that the entire family were incensed by the cruel behaviour, when Burns was only a boy, of a callous factor who demanded rent which William Burnes was unable to pay, and who wrote abusive letters. Burns could never forgive him. The death of his father triggered off a memory of shared impotent anger, coupled with fear, and the factor therefore 'sat for his picture' in 'The Twa Dogs':

	I've notic'd, on our Laird's *court-day*,
many sad	An' mony a time my heart's been wae,
-people short	Poor *tenant-bodies*, scant o' cash,
must bear abusive talk	How they maun thole a *factor*'s snash;
	He'll stamp an' threaten, curse an' swear,
seize property	He'll *apprehend* them, *poind* their gear,
must	While they maun stand, wi' aspect humble,
all	An' hear it a', an' fear an' tremble.

The portrait is of a type, worthy only of contempt. Burns might be writing in the white heat of remembered anger, but a rankling sense of injustice made him all the more determined to control his tone, and generalise his attack. Had he not seen in the last months of his father's life in 1783-4 another example of the hostility between the landlord class and a defenceless tenant, in this instance leading to a writ of sequestration, and accelerating William Burnes's death? Enough, then, by calling in doubt the actual gender of a laird's

> *Whipper-in*, wee blastet wonner,   huntsman   accursed
> Poor, worthless elf, it eats a dinner,
> Better than ony *Tenant-man*
> His Honor has in a' the lan'   all   land

to expose the mediocrity of the entire social category to which self-important factors belonged. He judged them to be less than complete human beings.

The basis of a good deal of Burns's satiric writing is personal. He wrote, as he spoke, about real individuals, whether or not he took the trouble to disguise their identity. Hence the number of epigrams in collected editions of his works. Many of these are trivial, and of no great poetic merit. But the capacity and edge show through, making good Maria Riddell's claim about his 'brilliant repartee'; often criticism of an individual becomes secondary to the play of wit. When Burns was in Edinburgh, for instance, 'he was introduced by a friend to a well-known painter, whom he found in his studio engaged on a picture of Jacob's dream; after minutely examining the work, he wrote the following verse on the back of a little sketch':

> Dear ——, I'll gie ye some advice.   give you
>   You'll tak it no uncivil: take not
> You shouldna paint at angels, man,
>   But try and paint the Devil.

> To paint an angel's kittle wark,   delicate work
>   Wi' Nick there's little danger;   Satan
> You'll easy draw a lang-kent face,   long-known
>   But no sae weel a stranger.   so well

The joke is a traditional one, which adds to its effectiveness.

While Burns produced many epigrams and personal *jeux d'esprits* of a satirical type, and engaged fiercely as a poet in Ayrshire ecclesiastical disputes, he wrote relatively few full-scale poetic satires which have stood the test of time. Part of the reason must be that he knew it was too risky for a poor countryman like himself to print poems which had as their butts particular known individuals, especially when he already had enemies enough in the church because of his sexual peccadilloes. This meant inevitably that the incentive to write finished satires was reduced. Instead, Burns enjoyed passing among his friends in manuscript poems which contained scathing comment on local affairs and personalities. As a young poet in Ayrshire, he took the opportunity to do this fairly often, sometimes distributing several copies of a recently written satire; and the practice was to continue when he went to live in Dumfriesshire and found himself reacting with amusement to local parliamentary elections. Discretion dictated his practice, as far as print was concerned. Undoubtedly he gained in freedom to be frank through *not* seeking to publish dangerous satires. At one level, however, he must have found it discouraging that formal publication was out of the question, because, as the Kilmarnock edition demonstrates, the prospect of appearing in 'guid black prent' stimulated him to write some of his most successful poetry.

Comparison between the satires included in the Kilmarnock *Poems* and a number of those left out of the volume illustrates both the principles by which Burns worked in seeking to communicate with a wider public, and the quality of his best omitted poems.

Outstanding among the satirical poems which he published in 1786 are 'The Twa Dogs' and 'The Holy Fair'. We have already seen that the first is indirect social satire, hard-hitting in content yet genial in tone. 'The

Holy Fair' for its part is arguably the finest of all Burns's church-related poems, a beautifully controlled send-up of the Mauchline summer Communion of 1785.

Behind this poem lies a long tradition of vernacular Scottish poetry describing social events. The most influential single model for the literary form handed down in modified guise to Burns is the mediaeval 'peasant brawl' poem, 'Christ's Kirk on the Green', usually ascribed to King James V (1513-1542). This presents the events of a single day at Christ's kirk, in a style which combines celebration with more than a hint of satire, and in a highly distinctive metre:

> Was never in Scotland hard nor sene
> Sic dansing nor deray,   disturbance
> Nother in Falkland on the grene,
> Nor in Peblis to the play,   Peebles
> As was of wowaris as I wene   suitors   think
> At Chrystis kirk on ane day.
> Thair come our Kittie wesching clene   washing
> In hir new kirtill of gray,
> Full gay,
> At Chrystis kirk on the grene.[4]

Among the many poets who contributed to the development of the 'Christis Kirk stanza' was Burns's immediate predecessor Robert Fergusson, whose 'Leith Races' is a deftly updated mid-eighteenth century urban equivalent of the 'peasant brawl' poem. Fergusson follows tradition in writing with his tongue in his cheek, yet without making the amusing scenes he describes obey a controlling satirical point of view. He introduces the presiding figure of Mirth — which was to give Burns a vital hint for 'The Holy Fair'. The emphasis in Fergusson's poem is very much on the comic and even farcical appearance and conduct of individual characters and groups, rather than on any widely shared hypocrisy, folly or human failing. Essentially, 'Leith Races' achieves its effects by describing the antics of a holiday crowd: the lubricant drink is unifying theme enough:

tinker fellows	The tinkler billies i' the Bow
busy hammering	Are now less eidant clinking,
long as strength allow	As lang's their pith or siller dow,
carrying on	They're daffin', and they're drinking
down crowds	Bedown Leith-Walk what burrochs reel
every	Of ilka trade and station,
make children	That gar their wives an' childer feel
empty stomachs	Toom weyms for their libation
these	O' drink thir days. . . .
go all out	The races o'er, they hale the dools,
of every kind	Wi' drink o'a' kin-kind;
part go limping home	Great feck gae hirpling hame like fools,
	The cripple lead the blind.
	May ne'er the canker o' the drink
perverse	E'er make our spirits thrawart,
	Case we git wharewitha' to wink
eyes bluebell	Wi' een as blue's a blawart
strokes	Wi' straiks thir days![5]

Between this poem and 'The Holy Fair' lies Burns's observation of a phenomenon particularly associated with the West of Scotland, namely a craze for country communions. These were breeding-grounds both of 'enthusiasm' in the eighteenth-century sense of fanatical zeal, and of uninhibited merry-making. The innovative power of Burns's poem derives from the fact that he knows his subject at firsthand, and holds to a consistent point of view. 'The Holy Fair' is full-blooded satire, turning on a contrast between professed and actual inclinations. Burns keeps all the main characteristics of the 'Leith Races' type of poem which simultaneously presents and gently sends up a particular social event, but invests the form with a quite new scope and cutting edge.

Mauchline in 1785 was a scene made for Burns's

powers of ridicule. Two years later, he explained to Dr
John Moore the nature of his motivation in the satires on
church affairs which date from this period. 'Polemical
divinity about this time was putting the country half-mad;
and I, ambitious of shining in conversation parties on
Sundays between sermons, funerals, &c. used . . . to
puzzle Calvinism with so much heat and indiscretion that
I raised a hue and cry of heresy against me which has not
ceased to this hour'. In 'The Holy Fair', his target is not
so much any single particular variety of polemical divinity
— although we are presented in the central section of the
poem with a selection of rival preachers — as the
hypocrisy shown on the kind of occasion which brought
together representatives of different theological per-
suasions and their untheologically minded adherents.

Burns does not exaggerate in suggesting that at a
summer communion large numbers of people were
involved. A Holy Fair went on for several days before
reaching its climax in the Communion service. Those
with an interest in taking part were prepared to travel
from far and wide to hear the 'preachings'. Mauchline
had only about 400 communicant church members, but it
is on record that in 1786 no fewer than 1,400 received the
sacrament, and it hardly seems likely that the publication
of Burns's *Poems* caused this number to be significantly
higher than on the second Sunday in August the year
before, the probable occasion of 'The Holy Fair'.
Someone of the next generation was to recall a typical
scene from the expanded Communion service at such a
time: 'One of the old stories I have heard of the
Mauchline communion is, that on one occasion a boy,
whom I remember as an old man . . . heard the beadle
call to the preacher in the tent, to "fire away, for the
seventeenth table was filling, and there was no end to the
work".'[6]

The poem begins not with the frenzied communal
scene, but instead in the open air, with the poet enjoying

the beauty and freshness of a calm Sunday morning, the single day when he does not have to work:

summer	Upon a simmer Sunday morn,
	When Nature's face is fair,
	I walked forth to view the corn,
fresh	An' snuff the callor air.
Moors	The rising sun, owre GALSTON Muirs,
glinting	Wi' glorious light was glintan;
hobbling ditches	The hares were hirplan down the furrs,
larks singing	The lav'rocks they were chantan
very	Fu' sweet that day.

In this way Burns establishes that he as narrator belongs to the world of Nature and instinctive living, which is soon to be contrasted with social artifice. He then adds to the reader's sense of anticipation by describing his meeting with a 'sweet lass', *Fun*, who immediately tells him that two miserable-looking figures travelling beside her are *Superstition* and *Hypocrisy*, and that all three are on their way to Mauchline Holy Fair . . .

going	"I'm gaun to Mauchline *holy fair*,
fooling	"To spend an hour in daffin:
if that wrinkled	'Gin ye'll go there, yon runkl'd pair,
	"We will get famous laughin
	At them this day".

The bond between Fun and Burns as narrator is one of pleasure in each other's company, and in shared 'remarkin'; but that they happen to be of opposite sexes clearly adds to the poet's zestful enjoyment of the occasion. His relationship with the laughing girl is deliberately presented as the most natural thing in the world, preparing the way for our amused recognition of the place of sex in country life later in the poem. One of the main positives of 'The Holy Fair', a male-female attraction, is not at this point contained by a repressive code, although Hypocrisy is already at hand; whereas later, the effect of a life-denying social code will be to provoke a riotously carnal reaction among younger members of the community.

That something of the kind lies ahead is indicated by the frankness of stanza IX, which provides a contrast to Mauchline's Sabbath morning respectability, by describing Janet Gibson, the half-witted daughter of 'Poosie Nansie', keeper of a disreputable tavern in the Cowgate, and her low life companions . . .

Here stands a shed to fend the showr's,
 An' screen our countra Gentry;   country
There, *racer Jess*, an' twathree wh-res, two or three
 Are blinkan at the entry.
Here sits a raw o' tittlan jads,   row gossiping wenches
 Wi' heaving breasts an' bare neck;
An' there, a batch o' *Wabster lads*, weaver
Blackguarding frae K[ilmarno]ck   from
  For *fun* this day.

'The Holy Fair' gains its effects in two ways; by presenting group scenes, and by focusing on particular individuals, through a technique which seems to point forward to the twentieth-century camera's zoom lens. The actual naming of 'Racer Jess' is a calculated affront to the douce folk of Mauchline. Cautiously, Burns indicates by initials only the identity of the succession of preachers in the tent, men like 'Black' Russell, and Willie Peebles, for whom he has scant respect:

For Peebles, frae the water-fit,   from -foot
 Ascends the *holy rostrum*:
See, up he's got the word o' G——,
 An' meek an' mim has view'd it,
While COMMON-SENSE has taen the taken
  road,
 An' aff, an' up the *Cowgate*   off
  Fast, fast that day.

(That this satiric portraiture had bite is shown by the fact that the Reverend William Peebles, a butt in more than one poem, never forgave Burns. In 1811, he published ragged, scornful verses attacking the Greenock Burns Club — the earliest of its kind — for perpetuating Burns's name:

> What call you this? It it Insania?
> I'll coin a word, 'tis Burnomania.
> His Greenock friends we therefore dub
> The Annual Burnomanian Club.[7])

Group scenes offer Burns an opportunity to introduce homely, down-to-earth humour which helps to ensure that the overall tone of the poem remains pleasantly relaxed:

> Here, some are thinkan on their sins,
> An' some upo' their claes;
> Ane curses feet that fyl'd his shins,
> Anither sighs an' prays

clothes   *claes*
one dirtied   *Ane curses feet that fyl'd his shins*
another   *Anither*

The subtle balancing of contrasts within these four lines is matched by the dexterity of the second half of the stanza, where he gives pride of place to one of his main targets, a huddle of the 'Elect', and then robs them of all dignity by mentioning in the very next breath 'a set of lads' with no more spiritual aim than to wink at the girls as they make for chairs:

> On this hand sits an *Elect* swatch,
> Wi' screw'd-up, grace-proud faces;
> On that, a set o' chaps, at watch,
> Thrang winkan on the lasses
> To *chairs* that day.

sample   *swatch*
busy   *Thrang*

In driving home his point about natural carnality prevailing over holy objectives, Burns is cheeky enough to parody a thought made familiar to generations of Scots through the metrical psalms. 'O happy is that man, an'

blest!', he writes . . . whose girl sits so close to him that
he is able to slip his arm round her and fondle her bosom
'unkend that day'. This, presumably while Psalm 146 is
being sung in the tent:

> O happy is that man and blest,
>   whom Jacob's God doth aid . . .
> Who made the earth and heavens high,
>   who made the swelling deep.

Oblique, but clear to readers familiar with Scottish
presbyterian practice, this sort of ironic allusion adds to
the boldness of Burns's satire in 'The Holy Fair'.
Cumulatively, the scenes which he describes have the
effect of emphasising sex and drink over against religiosity
as primary motivating human values even in professedly
holy Mauchline. He caps the poem by adding to his
extended series of contrasts between ostensibly holy aims
and actual human desires a final robustly suggestive
picture. Once more, there is a daring biblical reference, to
Ezekiel xxxvi, 26: 'A new heart also will I give you, and a
new spirit will I put within you: and I will take away the
stony heart out of your flesh, and I will give you an heart
of flesh'.:

How monie hearts this day converts,	many
O' sinners and o' Lasses!	
Their hearts o' stane, gin night are gane,	stone before gone
As saft as onie flesh is.	soft any
There's some are fou o' *love divine*;	full
There's some are fou o' *brandy*;	
An' monie jobs that day begin,	intrigues
May end in *Houghmagandie*	fornication
Some ither day.	other

A valuable and revealing early criticism of 'The Holy
Fair' is that by Scott's son-in-law J. G. Lockhart in his
1828 *Life* of Burns, 'This was, indeed, an extraordinary
performance; no partisan of any sect could whisper that

malice had formed its principal inspiration, or that its chief attraction lay in the boldness with which individuals, entitled and accustomed to respect, were held up to ridicule; it was acknowledged, amidst the sternest mutterings of wrath, that national manners were once more in the hands of a national poet; and hardly denied by those who shook their heads the most gravely over the indiscretions of particular passages, or even by those who justly regretted a too prevailing tone of levity in the treatment of a subject essentially solemn, that the Muse of "Christ's Kirk on the Green" had awakened, after the slumber of ages, with all the vigour of her regal youth, about her, in "the auld clay biggin' of Mossgiel".'[8]

'Holy Willie's Prayer' has an epigraph from Pope's 'Rape of the Lock': 'And send the godly in a pet to pray'. In August 1784 Burns's friend Gavin Hamilton was cited before the annual communion at Mauchline — the very event which would be satirised in 'The Holy Fair' — for his neglect of public worship. The case went on to the presbytery of Ayr, and in January 1785 the 'Moderates' in the presbytery succeeded in having the Mauchline session minute against Hamilton erased. The immediate occasion for 'Holy Willie's Prayer' was the Hamilton faction's rejoicing at the decision of Ayr presbytery. In an 'argument' introducing the poem, Burns alludes to the part played by a leading Mauchline elder, William Fisher, in the events leading up to the unsuccessful 'process' against Hamilton.:

> Holy Willie was a rather oldish batchelor Elder in the parish of Mauchline, and much and justly famed for that polemical chattering which ends in tippling Orthodoxy, and for that Spiritualized Bawdry which refines to Liquorish Devotion.— — In a Sessional process with a gentleman in Mauchline, a Mr Gavin Hamilton, Holy Willie, and his priest, father Auld, after a full hearing in the Presbytery of Ayr, came off but second best; owing partly to the oratorical powers

of M[r] Rob[t] Aiken, M[r] Hamilton's Counsel; but
chiefly to M[r] Hamilton's being one of the most
irreproachable and truly respectable characters in the
country. — On losing his Process, the Muse over-
heard him at his devotions as follows —

The careful construction of this headnote — virtually part
of the literary text, like the prose in some of Pope's satires
— shows that at some point Burns contemplated publication. On grounds of caution he decided against printing
the poem, contenting himself instead with the enthusiastic
response of his friends, to whom it was shown in manuscript — and with the knowledge that 'Holy Willie's
Prayer' succeeded in thoroughly irritating the kirk
session. He was to explain to Dr Moore that this poem

> annoyed the kirk-Session so much that they held
> three several meetings to look over their holy
> artillery, if any of it was pointed against profane
> Rhymers. Unluckily for me, my idle wanderings led
> me, on another side, point-blank within the reach of
> their heaviest metal . . .[9]

— a wry reference to the sexual misdemeanours for which
Burns was more than once summoned before the
Mauchline congregation.

The poem is a poised and sustained dramatic
monologue, of a quality to compare with any of
Browning's in English the following century. From the
beginning, Burns uses his familiarity with the idiom of
Scottish religious devotion and his mastery of verse form
to destroy Willie Fisher's character from within. Moreover, he makes Willie observe the ordered structure of
presbyterian prayer. Unconscious ironies abound. The
monologuist's confident invocation of his deity, sending
'ane to heaven and ten to h-ll', is quickly followed by a
gleeful meditation on the special purpose for which he,
Fisher, has been called to be

A burning and a shining light
To a' this place.

all

One of Burns's weapons is controlled juxtaposition. No
sooner has Willie congratulated himself on his role as
'ruler and example/To a' thy flock' than he begins to try
to 'get round' God by referring to his pardonable weaknesses of the flesh:

Yet I am here, a chosen sample,
To shew thy grace is great and ample:
I'm here, a pillar o' thy temple
    Strong as a rock,
A guide, a ruler and example
    To a' thy flock. —

But yet — O L——d — confess I must—
At times I'm fash'd wi' fleshly lust;
And sometimes too, in warldly trust
    Vile Self gets in;
But thou remembers we are dust,
    Defil'd wi' sin. —

troubled

This theme having been broached, Willie does not
hesitate to cleanse his conscience by off-loading the
troublesome particulars of his most recent minor lapse;
then he consoles himself further by bringing his prayer
back to the highway of general pious reflection. Perhaps
like St Paul he has been tested by having to contend with a
'thorn in the flesh'? Here the mixture of farming
language and the 'language of the saints' is particulary
lethal.

yesterday knows   O L—d yestreen — thou kens — wi'
                          Meg —
                     Thy pardon I sincerely beg!
                     O may't ne'er be a living plague,
                         To my dishonor!
                     And I'll ne'er lift a lawless leg
                         Again upon her. —

Besides, I farther maun avow,   *must*
Wi' Leezie's lass, three times — I trow —
But L—d, that friday I was fou   *drunk*
  When I cam hear her;
Or else, thou kens, thy servant true
  Wad never steer her. —

Maybe thou lets this fleshly thorn
Buffet thy servant e'en and morn,
Lest he o'er proud and high should turn,
  That he's sae gifted;   *so*
If sae, thy hand maun e'en be borne   *even*
  Untill thou lift it.

By the time he reaches the 'petition' section of his prayer, Willie has cleared out of the way everything which might inhibit his holy zeal against Gavin Hamilton:

L——d bless thy Chosen in this place,
For here thou has a chosen race:
But G—d, confound their stubborn face,
  And blast their name,
Wha brings thy rulers to disgrace
  And open shame. —

In naming his enemy, he gives vent to energetically personal denunciation. At this point the poem recalls both an Old Testament curse of the ungodly and an occasion when Hamilton was charged by the kirk session with causing his servant to pick potatoes on the Sabbath:

L—d mind Gaun Hamilton's deserts!   *Gavin*
He drinks, and swears, and plays at
    cartes,   *cards*
Yet has sae mony taking arts   *many*
  Wi' Great and Sma',   *Small*
Frae G—d's ain priest and people's hearts *own*
  He steals awa. —   *away*

And when we chasten'd him therefore,

such an uproar   Thou kens how he bred sic a splore

And set the warld in a roar
    O' laughin at us:
Curse thou his basket and his store,

kale   Kail and potatoes. —

The voice with which Willie prays becomes more and more spiteful as he asks for vengeance on Robert Aitken, the 'glib-tongu'd' lawyer who defended Hamilton in the Ayr Presbytery,

To think how I sat, sweating, shaking,
    And p—ss'd wi' dread.

Yet Willie is not so completely carried away as to forget to make a final request for his own present and future prosperity:

But L——d, remember me and mine
Wi' mercies temporal and divine!

property   That I for grace and gear may shine,
    Excell'd by nane!
And a' the glory shall be thine!
AMEN! AMEN!

Scott accurately described 'Holy Willie's Prayer' as 'exquisitely severe'. He commented understandingly in 1809 that James Currie presumably found it too 'daringly profane' to include in the first collected edition of Burns's Poems (1800): the strength of local reaction was obviously a factor which had to be taken into account by Burns's editor. On the other hand, Scott argued that there had been little justification for Currie's decision to omit from his edition 'Love And Liberty, a Cantata', otherwise known as 'The Jolly Beggars', in Scott's judgement an outstanding work, 'for humorous description and nice discrimination of character . . . inferior to no poem of the same length in the whole range of English poetry'.[10]

It was in fact merely by bad luck that 'Love and

Liberty' was left out of the 1787 edition of Burns's *Poems*. He wanted to publish it, and submitted a copy of what he had written to Hugh Blair, a leading Edinburgh critic and university professor, only to be met with the frosty comment that

> The Whole of What is called the Cantata, the Songs of the Beggars and their Doxies, with the Grace at the end of them, are altogether unfit in my opinion for publication. They are by much too licentious; and fall below the dignity which Mr Burns possesses in the rest of his poems & would rather degrade them.[11]

Thereafter Burns put the work aside, keeping no copy of his own. In 1793 when the music publisher George Thomson asked him about it, he claimed that he had completely forgotten 'Love and Liberty', except for the final song — which Blair had referred to as 'the Grace'. Fortunately, a copy which Burns had passed to a friend had found its way into print, ensuring its survival.

'Love and Liberty' presents what purports to be a direct visual and aural transcript of one night's convivial drinking by a company of beggars in Poosie Nansie's Inn in Mauchline in the autumn of 1785. Burns was present and composed the cantata not long afterwards. He had no closely analogous model with which to work, but it is clear that he drew certain ideas from traditional songs about beggars, and others from the popular ballad-operas which had been inspired by John Gay's *The Beggar's Opera* (1728). It seems obvious that he must have played over on his fiddle most of the tunes he used; yet he can have heard no complete performance of the cantata. In that sense, 'Love and Liberty' remained incomplete, a work to be enjoyed only in his imagination.

Like a number of Burns's other works, and like such mediaeval masterpieces as Henryson's 'Testament of Cresseid', 'Love and Liberty' opens (in 'The Cherrie and The Slae' stanza) by setting up a contrast between a hostile winter scene out of doors

striking force   when hailstanes drive wi' bitter skyte
                    And infant Frosts begin to bite,
hoar-frost   In hoary cranreuch drest

and a warm, congenial interior. But the beggars have
been driven to seek Nanse Tinnock's fireside by their
liking for a dram no less than by the ominous cold of a
November night. Their purpose is to enjoy a 'splore' or
noisy exchange of words and songs, and to get very
drunk. As time goes past, they will express their identity
physically and aggressively. Straightaway, we are
informed that they have come together 'to drink their orra
duddies' — in other words to pay for what they drink with
the less essential clothes they have been able to beg. They
are 'randie, gangrel bodies', vagrants and riotous
outcasts from respectable society.

   In keeping with the mood of the opening, the songs and
passages of recitative which follow in alternating sequence
are designed to convey the idea of intense physicality, of
rough and anarchic *life*. While telling their case-stories in
song, certain of the beggars use a kind of 'anti-language',
parodying the idiom of polite society; and none hesitates
to pour scorn in passing on those who let them down. The
tipsy 'martial Chuck', for instance, who has slept with
half the regiment, and who has now been reduced by 'the
Peace' — the Peace of Versailles of 1783 — to beg in
despair at Cunningham fair, makes it plain in a lyric style
mocking the romantic that she was set on this path by an
army chaplain, who ought to have protected her:

              The first of my LOVES was a swaggering
                 blade,
              To rattle the thundering drum was his
                 trade;
              His leg was to tight and his cheek was so
                 ruddy,
soldier   Transported I was with my SODGER
                 LADDIE.

But the godly old Chaplain left him in the
    lurch,
The sword I forsook for the sake of the
    church;
He ventur'd the SOUL, and I risked the
    BODY,
'Twas then I proved false to my
    SODGER LADDIE.

Burns's implication is clear. Those who have been
rejected by society were first exploited by their social
'betters', the representatives of law and religion.
Somehow they want to get their own back. After much
incidental comedy has been presented in the amorous
words and actions of rival beggars — skilfully varied and
entertaining by-play to the cantata's wider meaning, or in
an alternative reading its central content — Burns returns
to the theme of social rejection. This time, through the
second song of a beggar poet, significantly in English to
make the ideas universally understood, he sums up the
defiant attitude of the beggars as a whole. Their code may
not be that of church or law-court, but that does not
trouble them in the least. Their stance is one of radical
and utter opposition to everything approved — as they
would have it, repressed — by conventional society. They
opt for what they see as the freedom of anarchy:

SEE the smoking bowl before us,
    Mark our jovial, ragged ring!
Round and round take up the Chorus,
    And in raptures let us sing —

Chorus

A fig for those by law protected!
    LIBERTY's a glorious feast!
Courts for Cowards were erected,
    Churches built to please the PRIEST.

What is TITLE, what is TREASURE,
　　What is REPUTATION's care?
If we lead a life of pleasure,
　　'Tis no matter HOW or WHERE.
　　　　A fig, &c.

With the ready trick and fable,
　　Round we wander all the day;
And at night, in barn or stable,

wenches　　Hug our doxies on the hay.
　　　　A fig for &c.

Does the train-attended CARRIAGE
　　Thro' the country lighter rove?
Does the sober bed of MARRIAGE
　　Witness brighter scenes of love?
　　　　A fig for &c.

Life is all a VARIORUM,
　　We regard not how it goes;
Let them chant about DECORUM,
　　Who have character to lose.
　　　　A fig for &c.

Here's to BUDGETS, BAGS AND
　　　　WALLETS!
　　Here's to all the wandering train!
Here's our ragged BRATS and

wenches　　　　CALLETS!
　　One and all cry out, AMEN!
　　A fig for those by LAW protected,
　　　　LIBERTY's a glorious feast!
Courts for Cowards were erected,
　　CHURCHES built to please the Priest.

　　Burns's artistic purpose in 'Love and Liberty'
obviously includes conveying the characteristic appearance, behaviour, and outlook of the beggars who join in

this chorus: he seeks to depict how the 'other half' lives. Some would argue that he has created a robustly amusing rather than an overtly satiric and political ending to the cantata. But melody, the human voice, and crescendo all come into play, heightening the social criticism which his words express. The only work of the later eighteenth century which can be set beside 'Life and Liberty' is Blake's ironic exposé of establishment ideas in *The Marriage Of Heaven And Hell* (1790). Two of the 'Proverbs of Hell' in that work succinctly express the outlook of Burns's beggars: 'Damn braces: bless relaxes', 'Energy is eternal delight'. In its overall direction, as well as its verbal content, 'Life and Liberty' shows in Burns a capacity for rendering man's unofficial self, and the angry, finger-to-nose feelings of all who are disadvantaged and made to wander from village to village with no better prospect than to seek temporary oblivion through drink. It is the work of a born satirist who understands how to link words and melody with dramatic effect.

NOTES

1 *Burns As Others Saw Him*, ed. W. L. Renwick (Edinburgh, 1959), p. 1-2.

2 *Ibid.*, p. 4.

3 *Robert Burns: The Critical Heritage*, ed. D. A. Low (1974), p. 104.

4 'Christ's Kirk on the Green', ll. 1-10, *Oxford Book of Scottish Verse*, ed. John MacQueen and Tom Scott (1966), p. 195.

5 'Leith Races', ll. 91-99, 172-180, *Poems by Allan Ramsay and Robert Fergusson*, ed. A. M. Kinghorn and A. Law (1974), pp. 176-7, 179.

6 Quoted in *Poems And Songs of Robert Burns*, ed. James Kinsley (Oxford, 1968), vol. 3, p. 1094.

7 *Robert Burns: The Critical Heritage*, p. 251.

8 J. G. Lockhart, *Life of Robert Burns* (3rd ed., 'corrected', 1830), pp. 71-2.

9 *Letters of Robert Burns*, ed. J. De Lancey Ferguson and G. Ross Roy (Oxford, 1985), I, 144, 2 August 1787 to Dr John Moore.

10 See D. A. Low, 'Scott's criticism of "The Jolly Beggars",' *Bibliotheck* 5 (6), 1969, pp. 207-9.

11 *Robert Burns: The Critical Heritage*, p. 82.

CHAPTER 4

TWO TALES

In Burns's Ayrshire, a social custom which helped to shorten long winter evenings was the event known as a 'rocking'. A number of people who lived near one another came together in somebody's house and enjoyed a *ceilidh*, exchanging news, stories, and songs. They might also spin or do other work of the kind; in such a gathering the time flew. John Sheppard, a minister of Muirkirk, described a rocking as taking place

> when neighbours visit one another in pairs, or threes or more in company, during the moonlight of winter or spring . . . The custom seems to have arisen when spinning on the *rock* or *distaff* was in use, which therefore was carried along with the visitant to a neighbour's house, [and] still prevails, though the rock is laid aside.[1]

Burns gives a vivid glimpse of an evening of this kind in his first 'Epistle to Lapraik'. The particular rocking he writes of took place on Shrove Tuesday in 1785:

Shrove Tuesday, spinning-party	On Fasteneen we had a rocking,
have a chat	To ca' the crack and weave our stocki⟩
	And there was muckle fun and jokin
	Ye need na doubt;
set-to	At length we had a hearty yokin,
singing in turn	At *sang about*.

He goes on to explain that one song pleased him above the rest, and when he inquired who had written it, he was told it was by 'an odd kind chiel about Muirkirk'. So he learned of the existence of John Lapraik.

The first 'Epistle to Lapraik' reveals how passionate was Burns's interest in poetry. It was typical of him to show curiosity about a fellow Ayrshire bard: he used up shoe leather and ink in making fast a friendship with Lapraik, who as it happens had fallen on bad times and appreciated his kindness all the more for that reason. But the poem also throws light on the kind of writer Burns was in another way, by its deft indication of what went on at the rocking. The occasion was a genuinely communal one, expressing the interests shared by farming folk. Burns belonged to a society which relished personality, fun and joking, and local incident. To 'ca' the crack' was to chat or gossip about people, their doings, and eccentricities. Quite possibly, Burns learned a good deal about that 'very worthy facetious old fellow', Lapraik, there and then, on Fasteneen. A strong taste for 'character' and a fund of anecdote and miscellaneous information existed along with a love of fiddle music and song in the community of which Burns was a member. It is easy to imagine that when neighbours met, as often as not the poet was the life and soul of the company; for not only did he have the precious gift of song-writing, he was, additionally, an expert and humorous observer of human nature, deeply versed in its most amusing local variations.

This is the essential background of most of Burns's poetry. He was above all else a natural communicator, who worked with rather than against the bias of circumstances, and what he sought to communicate had a direct appeal to men and women from the same rural society as himself. That his poems reached out to a wider public beyond Ayrshire was in a sense quite accidental, and remains so. He had read widely, it is true, and could amuse himself by imitating and even surpassing the literary artifice of bookish men; and like other young poets, he was ambitious for fame. But all this was secon-

dary. Burns was most universal when writing about what
he knew and experienced at firsthand. He drew his main
creative inspiration from his own people, returning with
generous interest to that living source in their own
language what he had received from boyhood onwards.
The result was that when the Kilmarnock edition was
published in 1786, throughout southwestern Scotland 'old
and young, high and low, grave and gay, learned or
ignorant, all were alike delighted'.[2]

Many of the poems flowed from real-life situations in
which Burns had been involved, and concerned actual,
identifiable individuals, even if only as a starting-point or
in passing. Part of the pleasure for those who first heard
or read his work, was to learn how he had 'taken off', in
satire or celebration, persons known to themselves.
However, in the process of composition, the local,
particularised, real-life elements were caught up in the
poet's imagination and transformed, as his two fully
developed narrative poems show.[3]

The fame of Burns's second tale has almost entirely
eclipsed that of the first. He himself stated somewhat ruefully that 'Tam o' Shanter' was his 'standard performance in the poetical line'. Traditionally this brilliant and
popular poem has been discussed on its own; but 'Tam o'
Shanter' appears in a new light when placed beside
'Death and Doctor Hornbook', the merits of which
deserve to be better known.

Burns married in the period which intervened between
the two poems. One reason for the popularity of 'Tam o'
Shanter' is that it has a new dimension of humour, that of
sexual relationships. There are the references to Tam's
wife waiting at home, to the landlady's favours 'secret,
sweet, and precious', and to the witches:

> Now, *Tam,* O *Tam*! had they been
girls   queans,
> A' plump and strapping in their teens . . .

The sexual comedy provides the supreme event in the tale:

> Even Satan glowr'd, and fidg'd fu' fain, twitched excitedly
> And hotch'd and blew wi' might and
>   main:
> Till first ae caper, syne anither, then
> *Tam* tint his reason a' thegither, lost completely
> And roars out, 'Weel done, Cutty-sark!'

This rollicking humour of physical desire transforms the atmosphere of 'Tam o' Shanter', and helps to universalise the fable.

'Death and Doctor Hornbook' was written in 1785, 'Tam o' Shanter' not until 1790. The first poem was conceived as a satire, the second as an extended illustration of the legend of Alloway Kirk. But although the two poems were produced by very different occasions, and separated by this long interval, they have a surprising amount in common. Both are comic tales about a drunken hero who meets Something on his way home at night. 'Death and Doctor Hornbook' is, on one level, a personal satire or lampoon on the character of 'Jock Hornbook', but it is also a poem which mocks at the idea of Death by robbing it of terror and solemnity. 'Tam o' Shanter' is primarily a comic tale. It corresponds to the earlier poem in that it once again incidentally reduces the dignity of a supernatural power, this time the Devil.

The two tales operate within similar limits. The most obvious technical difference between them is that 'Death and Doctor Hornbook' is a first person narrative while 'Tam o' Shanter' is a third person narrative. This difference between dramatic monologue and 'external' narrative is radical, and one of the subtlest features of 'Tam o' Shanter' is that most of the action is viewed through the eyes of a 'crony narrator' with a fondness for moralising (in English). Despite this, there is a clear similarity in treatment of the subject between the poems.

Fundamental to the succes of each is the projection of the character of the intoxicated hero. The exhibition of his credulous personality and heightened state of consciousness is in each case the 'action' before the action proper, building up suspense and making possible both unusual narrative economy at the climax and an ironic conclusion. In other words, the hero holds the tale together, rather than events.

It is tempting to identify as the matrix of 'Death and Doctor Hornbook' a brief poem 'On Tam the Chapman', which was first collected in the Aldine edition of Burns in 1839:

> As Tam the chapman on a day
> Wi' Death forgather'd by the way,
> Weel pleased, he greets a wight sae
>   famous,
> And Death was nae less pleas'd wi'
>   Thomas,
> Wha cheerfully lays down his pack,
> And there blaws up a hearty crack:
> His social, friendly, honest heart
> Sae tickled Death, they could na part;
> Sae after viewing knives and garters,
> Death taks him hame to gie him quarters.
>   [Kinsley no. 56]

begins   gossip

Neither Burns's authorship of these lines nor their date of composition is certainly established: but internal evidence strongly supports Professor Kinsley's view that 'On Tam the Chapman' belongs with Burns's poems of 1785.[4] Kinsley prints it immediately after 'Death and Doctor Hornbook'. But these lines read like a first sketch of the comic situation which was fully developed in 'Death and Doctor Hornbook'.

Admittedly, the fragment does no more than outline an encounter between the 'social, friendly' chapman and Death, and the ending is different; there can be no proof that the shorter poem was written first. However, the essence of the unexpected supernatural meeting described in 'Death and Doctor Hornbook' is found here, while the characters of Tam the chapman and of Death appear to foreshadow those in the verse tale. A poet is presumably more likely to develop a situation and characters from an initial brief draft than to base a fragmentary sketch upon an idea worked out in a long poem. The difference in the ending can be explained as something which is very common in Burns — a result of inspiration during the act of writing a long poem (compare any of the epistles). It seems probable that the hero's escape from Death, who promises

> 'Niest time we meet, I'll wad a groat,   next   wager small silver coin
> He gets his fairin''   what he deserves

was one of the many artistic ironies which suggested itself to the poet while he was actually at work on 'Death and Doctor Hornbook'.

Whether or not they were written first, the lines 'On Tam the Chapman' provide a remarkable analogue to the traveller's 'news' with Death in 'Death and Doctor Hornbook'. Their interest extends beyond this. The chapman's name, and his sociable garrulous nature both recur in 'Tam o' Shanter'. These common features may be rejected as having no particular significance. Burns's two allusions to chapmen in 'Tam o' Shanter' —

> When chapman billies leave the street

and

> By this time he was cross the ford,
> Where, in the snaw, the chapman
>   smoor'd   was smothered

can also be dismissed as coincidental similarities. It is more reasonable to assume, however, that in writing his comic masterpiece Burns drew for a second time on his

original theme of the open-hearted chapman who met
Something by the wayside.

The lines 'On Tam the Chapman' contain the first elements of characterisation and the central incident of a
supernatural folk-tale. Burns made use of the idea more
than once because of its power and quality as a folk-motif.
Drink was prominently introduced into both tales as a
catalyst of the comedy, but the trusting character of the
hero provided the basis of comic incongruity in his
meeting with the supernatural.

Most modern readers, standing outside Burns's kind of
oral tradition, indiscriminately categorise various kinds of
supernatural tales as 'ghost stories'. Burns's attitude was
very different. As he informed Dr Moore in his autobiographical letter of August 1787, his interest in the supernatural began in childhood. He distinguished among
supernatural *phenomena* with a cool analytical skill which
any folk-lorist or scientific investigator might envy. Yet
even in doing so, he admitted to being so close to popular
superstition that it could prey on his imagination when he
was alone and off guard:

> In my infant and boyish days, too, I owned much to
> an old Maid of my Mother's, remarkable for her
> ignorance, credulity and superstition. — She had, I
> suppose, the largest collection in the country of tales
> and songs concerning devils, ghosts, fairies,
> brownies, witches, warlocks, spunkies, kelpies, elf-
> candles, deadlights, wraiths, apparitions, cantraips,
> giants, inchanted towers, dragons and other
> trumpery. — This cultivated the latent seeds of
> Poesy; but had so strong an effect on my imagina-
> tion, that to this hour, in my nocturnal rambles, I
> sometimes keep a sharp look-out in superstitious
> places; and though nobody can be more sceptical in
> these matters than I, yet it often takes an effort of
> Philosophy to shake off these idle terrors.[5]

This confession proves that Burns was directly affected by country superstitions to the point of sharing their 'terrors'; that he was nevertheless sceptical about the nature of the experiences on which they were based; and that he found them a fine subject for poetry. In 'Halloween' he attempted to present a kind of living museum of such folk-lore, which would be true to the 'manners' and the language of his part of Ayrshire and at the same time instructive and entertaining to people who did not share his knowledge of rural customs. The poem succeeds in its purpose of description, but lacks the spontaneous development of folk-tale. Burns was able to express his complex enjoyment of superstition much more fully in his verse tales, where he was freed from the self-imposed responsibility of comprehensive 'manners-painting'. Instead of maintaining a steady semi-sociological detachment, he could enter freely into the mythopoeic — and tipsy — state of mind of his hero. Thus 'Tam o' Shanter' would be praised by Coleridge for its 'freshness of sensation', for carrying on the feelings of childhood into the powers of manhood. But paradoxically, Burns's adoption of the seemingly artless narrative form of folk-tale, which released so much imaginative power within him, also allowed him to convey his ironic vision of superstitious man. It was only when he based his poetry on oral and popular models that he managed to fulfil his aesthetic aim without diminishing the human identity of his material. Every gift was then given expression, and the poetry which resulted was at once more immediately communicative and more subtle in its art.

'Death and Doctor Hornbook' has the narrative energy and deceptive surface simplicity of folk-tale. Formally, on the other hand, it is a satire cast in the *genre* of dramatic monologue. Burns thus combines in the same poem features which might appear to be wildly heterogeneous. He is able to do this because he is completely at ease in his use of the 'Standart Habby' stanza. There is not one monologuist, but two, and the primary satire is directed by the words of the second at a third figure, 'Hornbook' the quack. Hornbook does not speak in his own person, is not allowed to. Instead Death reveals his offences against linguistic and natural decorum by listing some of the names of his medicines and describing his notorious therapy. When he is first mentioned — which is not until line 77 — Burns has a footnote placing him as a satirical target. Its function is similar to that of the 'Argument' in 'Holy Willie's Prayer', but this time the language is mock-heroic, simultaneously parodying and distancing '*Jock Hornbook* i' the Clachan';

> This gentleman, Dr Hornbook, is, professionally, a brother of the sovereign Order of the Ferula; but, by intuition and inspiration, is at once an Apothecary, Surgeon, and Physician.

The prose comment is again integrated into the satire. Along with the dominie's nick-name (a hornbook was something every eighteenth-century beginner at school knew), and the acquired lingo of his second profession

—   Their Latin names as fast he rattles
     As A B C

—   Burns's phrase 'the sovereign Order of the Ferula' identifies Hornbook as an authority figure, and moreover a fraudulent one. As such, he is fair game.

Gilbert Burns's account of the origin of 'Death and Doctor Hornbook' suggests that the first monologuist is, quite simply, the poet. Remembering that his brother had spoken of a moment of inspiration during a solitary walk home at the end of a masonic evening spent in the company of the schoolmaster John Wilson, Gilbert wrote,

> at the place where he describes his meeting with Death, one of those floating ideas of apparition he

mentions in his letter to Dr Moore, crossed his mind;
this set him to work.[6]

There is perhaps nothing inherently implausible in this
version of how the supernatural and satirical themes first
came together in Burns's mind. But the words 'where he
describes his meeting with Death' obscure a crucial
distinction. The character in the poem who meets Death
is based in part on the poet's own, but he is also a *persona*,
whose failings are viewed sardonically, like those of Holy
Willie himself. The mockery is kinder and less obvious in
this poem because the traveller's kind of self-deception is
more sociable than Holy Willie's. Yet he has something of
the spiteful nature of a parish-pump gossip, as well as the
gullibility of Tam the Chapman.

Much of the pleasure of listening to gossip and funny
stories is in noticing how they reveal the shortcomings or
oddities of outlook of the story-teller. And if a man tells a
story against himself he earns a right to tell one against
somebody else. The traveller who staggers home by the
light of the moon gives away his weaknesses, and so does
Death. The reader is entertained not only by the
nefarious dealings of Hornbook, but by the fact that
Hornbook is seen through the envious eyes of Death; and
Death in turn is viewed by a drunken gossip who wants to
know all about everyone:

'Guid-een', quo' I; 'Friend! hae ye been
    mawin,   mowing
'When ither folk are busy sawin?'   sowing

A possible criticism of the poem is that the 'objective'
satire of Hornbook is too long delayed. Burns's remark
that he thought the poem 'too prolix' may indicate that he
himself took this view. But the quality of any tale is
largely determined by the build-up and incidentals which
precede the climax; and in this poem these features are
comparable with anything in Chaucer or Byron in terms

G

of wit, irony, and sheer entertainment. The traveller's initial protestation that what he has to say is true — and the subtitle 'A True Story' — serve the poet's purpose. Burns knows exactly how to confuse any attempt to decide whether or not his hero is what systematic critics of fiction call a Reliable Narrator. The traveller reveals idiosyncratic views straightaway, some would say bias:

known   Ev'n Ministers they hae been kenn'd,
          In holy rapture,
lie   A rousing whid, at times, to vend,
          And nail't wi' Scripture.
going   But this that I am gaun to tell,
        Which lately on a night befel,
        Is just as true's the Deil's in h—ll,
          Or Dublin city.

Swiftly, the poem passes to circumstantial narration. It is clear at least that the traveller has had an unusual Experience. Wordsworth greatly admired Burns's art in discriminating between the states of alcoholic illumination and intoxication. Rather solemnly, he explained:

> Burns at this time had very rarely been intoxicated, or perhaps even much exhilarated by liquor. Yet how happily does he lead his reader into that track of sensations! and with what lively humour does he describe the disorder of his senses and the confusion of his understanding, put to test by a deliberate attempt to count the horns of the moon! Behold a sudden apparition that disperses the disorder, and in a moment chills him into possession of himself. Coming upon no more important mission than the grisly phantom was charged with, what mode of introduction could have been more efficient or appropriate.[7]

Much more exciting, though, than Wordsworth's decision to imitate the unsteady return home in

'Benjamin   the   Waggoner',   was   to   be   Hugh
MacDiarmid's choice of the traveller's commentary-on-
his-progress as a guiding thread in *A Drunk Man Looks At
The Thistle*:

> It's no that I'm sae fou' as juist deid
>   dune,   drunk
> And dinna ken as muckle's whar I am
> Or hoo I've come to sprawl here 'neth the
>   mune.
> That's it! It isna me that's fou' at a',
> But the fu' mune, the doited jade, that's
>   led   crazed
> Me fer agley, or 'mogrified the warld.   astray

MacDiarmid seized on Burns's use of tipsiness as a way of
capturing the topsy-turvy disorder of the cosmos, and
made it his own.

In Burns's poem, Death ignores the traveller's
threatening bluster, then accepts his invitation to give his
'news'. He is true to the chronology of the catechism in
beginning a monologue the tone of which is that of outraged professional pride:

> Sax thousand years are near hand fled
> 'Sin I was to the butching bred,
> 'And mony a scheme in vain's been laid,
>   'To stap or scar me;
> 'Till ane Hornbook's ta'en up the trade,
>   'And faith, he'll waur me.   get the better of

He speaks like an undertaker cheated of the business
which is his due. And it is natural that he should pass on
to an exasperated catalogue of Hornbook's cures.

By this stage, the traveller has fulfilled his main role in
the poem; Burns has 'changed horses' from the first to the
second monologuist. He proceeds to create comic and
satiric effects at the expense both of Death and of
Hornbook. Some of these are splendidly direct and simple

in humorous content (e.g. lls. 109-114); others depend upon a combination of coarseness and sophisticated literary irony (e.g. lls. 85-90); still others, upon rapid linguistic transitions which give away the game of Hornbook's abracadabra (e.g. lls. 127-131). Burns guards against the danger that the satire may become too generalised, thereby losing its force, by introducing an element of symmetrical structural planning. Death has described Hornbook's efforts to save lives. The credulous traveller interrupts with apparent solicitude:

alas

> 'Waes me for *Johnny Ged's-Hole* now,'
> Quoth I, 'if that thae news be true!
> 'His braw calf-ward whare gowans grew,
>   'Sae white an' bonie,
> 'Nae doubt they'll rive it wi' the plew;
>   'They'll ruin *Johnie!*'

He need not fear, Death replies, with an eldritch laugh — Hornbook kills off many more than he saves! He launches into a gleeful description of Hornbook's thoroughly successful invasions into his own previous monopoly:

colic

rumbling

yearling ewes

> 'A countra Laird had ta'en the batts,
> Or some curmurring in his guts,
> His only son for *Hornbook* sets,
>   And pays him well,
> The lad, for twa guid gimmer-pets
>   Was Laird himsel.

After being described as formidable, Hornbook is laughed to scorn. The general formula of building up a victim, and then destroying him, is found in many satires by Dryden, Samuel Garth, Pope, and other English verse satirists whose work Burns had read. There is evidence to suggest that Garth's poem *The Dispensary* supplied Burns with more than one idea for 'Death and Doctor Hornbook'; and Sterne's characterisation of Doctor Slop contributed something also. But the interplay of folk-

humour and double-edged irony with minor echoes from
Augustan satire is unlike anything produced by an earlier
eighteenth-century satirist. Indeed, to find a parallel to
Burns's narrative technique in this poem, it is necessary
to turn to a twentieth-century novelist, Lewis Grassic
Gibbon. In Gibbon's short stories, and in his best work in
A Scots Quair, especially 'Sunset Song', dramatic speech is
used to satirise both the speaker and those he speaks
about. In the following extract, the comedy is primarily
directed outwards, at the expense of Munro, but the last
sentence brings out that there is also a vein of irony
(which runs throughout) exposing the prejudiced view of
the undefined teller of the tale, the 'voice' of the region:

> Well, Peesie's Knapp and Blawearie were the
> steadings that lay Stonehaven way. But if you turned
> east that winter along the Auchinblay road first on
> your right was Cuddiestoun, a small bit holding the
> size of Peesie's Knapp and old as it, a croft from the
> far-off times. It lay a quarter-mile or so from the
> main road and its own road was fair clamjamfried
> with glaur from late in the harvest till the coming of
> Spring. Some said maybe that accounted for
> Munro's neck, he could never get the glaur washed
> out of it. But others said he never tried. He was on a
> thirteen years' lease there, Munro, a creature from
> down south, Dundee way, and he was a good six feet
> in height but awful coarse among the legs, like a
> lamb with water on the brain, and he had meikle feet
> that seemed aye in his way. He was maybe forty
> years or so in age, and bald already, and his skin was
> red and creased in cheeks and chin and God! you
> never saw an uglier brute, poor stock.[8]

Any comparison between Burns and Lewis Grassic
Gibbon is inevitably general, but the heritage of folk
narrative skill endued with an extra gloss and ironical
tone is common to the two. Grassic Gibbon alone of

Burns's Scottish successors has fully caught the satirical nuances, and the lyrical flow, of reminiscent country speech.

In the end, 'Death and Doctor Hornbook' goes beyond specific satire to a level which allows the poet to demonstrate the folly of everybody, and the triviality of Death. As a supernatural tale, the poem lacks the varied comic resonance of 'Tam o' Shanter'; and 'Holy Willie's Prayer' surpasses it as a dramatic monologue: in each instance, the antics of man the amorous creature provide a source of laughter which is only glanced at in 'Death and Doctor Hornbook'. But it is nevertheless an ambitious, complex, and successful poem, one which illustrates among other things a couplet of the medically minded Garth:

> The wise, through thought th' insults of
>   death defy;
> The fools, through blest insensibility.

'Tam o' Shanter' is recited from memory or read aloud on Burns's birthday every year the world over — the finest possible tribute to a poem which draws directly on oral tradition. Save for the 'witch stories' Burns had heard about Alloway Kirk, and save for Francis Grose, who asked the poet to send him one of these, 'Tam o' Shanter' would never have been written. Grose, a notably quick-witted, convivial person, entered Burns's life in 1789, a year after the poet had moved from Ayrshire to Ellisland, near Dumfries. The two men met while Grose was staying for some weeks with Burns's friends the Riddells at Friar's Carse, and beginning to gather material for a work on Scottish antiquities, to be illustrated by himself, which would enable him to follow up the success of his *Antiquities of England and Wales* (1773-87). According to Gilbert Burns, the antiquarian and the poet were 'unco pack and thick thegither'. Among much that they had in common was a shared interest in the racier forms of speech, Grose having recently published a pioneering *Classical Dictionary of The Vulgar Tongue.*

Burns still looked on himself to some extent as an incomer in the county in which he now lived, but when Grose asked for information about old buildings and places of historic interest in Ayrshire, he supplied an itinerary and wrote to Mrs Dunlop of Dunlop to warn her that she might soon come across

> an old, fat fellow, the precise figure of Dr Slop, wheeling about your avenue in his own carriage with a pencil & paper in his hand.[9]

For the poet, Ayrshire carried all the associations of childhood and his first home. On moving south, he had begun an epistle to an Ayrshire friend with the words 'in this strange land, this uncouth clime . . .', revealingly if also playfully. He at once warmed to the theme of Grose's intended journey among places he knew so well, and, in his brother's words,

> Robert requested of Captain Grose, when he should come to Ayrshire, that he would make a drawing of Alloway-Kirk, as it was the burial-place of his father, and where he himself had a sort of claim to lay down his bones . . . and added, by way of encouragement, that it was the scene of many a good story of witches and apparitions, of which he knew the Captain was very fond. The Captain agreed to the request, provided the poet would furnish a witchstory, to be printed along with it. *Tam o' Shanter* was produced on this occasion.[10]

Gilbert Burns's note is helpful, but compresses chronology: 'Tam o' Shanter' was not written until late in 1790. What Burns did produce straightaway was a spirited poem 'on the Late Captain Grose's Peregrinations thro' Scotland, collecting the Antiquities of that Kingdom'. In this poem, which was published in the

Edinburgh Evening Courant in August 1789, Burns issued a
mock-warning to his fellow countrymen:

lad

> A chiel's amang you, taking notes,
>   And, faith, he'll prent it.

Clearly, witch stories had been much in the poet's mind,
because he provided an entertaining description of how
Grose might be detected pursing his researches among
ruins and in the wrong sort of company . . .

owl-, building

> By some auld, houlet-haunted, biggin,
> Or kirk deserted by its riggin,
> It's ten to ane ye'll find him snug in
>   Some eldritch part,
> Wi' deils, they say, L—d safe's!

save us

>   colleaguin
>   At some black art.

each, bed-chamber

> Ilk ghaist that haunts auld ha' or chamer,
> Ye gipsy-gang that deal in glamor,
> And you, deep-read in hell's black
>   grammar,
>   Warlocks and witches;
> Ye'll quake at his conjuring hammer,
>   Ye midnight b—es.

Burns was merely pulling Grose's leg here, but a year
later he was to put the idea behind these stanzas to fresh
use.

In June 1790, he wrote to Grose summarising the only
three stories about witches at Alloway Kirk which he
'distinctly' remembered; he implied that he had heard
and forgotten others. The third story, a local variant of an
international folk tale, has no close connection with 'Tam
o' Shanter', but the first, about a benighted ploughman,
supplied Burns with the setting of a storm and one or two
other details, and the second story, concerning a Carrick
farmer, was what he went to work on in writing his poem:

On a market day in the town of Ayr, a farmer from Carrick, and consequently whose way lay by the very gate of Aloway kirk-yeard, in order to cross the river Doon at the old bridge, which is about two or three hundred yards further on than the said gate, had been detained by his business till by the time he reached Aloway it was the wizard hour, between night and morning.

Though he was terrified with a blaze streaming from the kirk, yet as it is a well known fact, that to turn back on these occasions is running by far the greatest risk of mischief, he prudently advanced on his road. When he had reached the gate of the kirk-yeard, he was surprised and entertained, through the ribs and arches of an old gothic window which still faces the highway, to see a dance of witches merrily footing it round their old sooty blackguard master, who was keeping them all alive with the power of his bagpipe. The farmer stopping his horse to observe them a little, could plainly descry the faces of many old women of his acquaintance and neighbourhood. How the gentleman was dressed, tradition does not say; but the ladies were all in their smocks; and one of them happening unluckily to have a smock which was considerably too short to answer all the purpose of that piece of dress, our farmer was so tickled that he involuntarily burst out, with a loud laugh, ''Weel luppen, Maggy wi' the short sark!'' and recollecting himself instantly spurred his horse to the top of his speed. I need not mention the universally known fact, that no diabolical power can pursue you beyond the middle of a running stream. Lucky it was for the poor farmer that the river Doon was so near, for notwith-standing the speed of his horse, which was a good one, against he reached the middle of the arch of the bridge, and consequently the middle of the stream, the pursuing, vengeful hags were so close at his heels, that one of them actually sprung to seize him: but it was too late; nothing was on her side of the stream but the horse's tail, which immediately gave way to her infernal grip, as if blasted by a stroke of lightning; but the farmer was beyond her reach. — However, the unsightly, tail-less condition of the vigorous steed was to the last hours of the noble creature's life, an awful warning to the Carrick farmers, not to stay too late in Ayr markets.[11]

It is of interest that Byron's 'Beppo', the only verse tale by a British poet of the next fifty years to stand comparison with 'Tam o' Shanter', followed the same pattern of creation. First came a letter outlining the story to a friend — in Byron's case, the publisher, John Murray — and not long afterwards, the poem itself. In each case, setting down an outline of the situation in prose seems to have helped to clarify the poet's ideas and liberate his imagination. Burns sent part of his poem to Mrs Dunlop in November 1790, and the completed narrative to Grose on 1 December 1790. 'Tam o' Shanter' is unique among poems of its quality in that its first book-publication was as a footnote, in the second volume of Grose's *Antiquities of Scotland* (1791).

While Burns was stimulated to write 'Tam o' Shanter' by a powerful oral tradition which was still fresh in his memory, he also made use of another kind of popular source, the chapbook. Like countless other people throughout Scotland in the late eighteenth century, he was familiar with the chapbook stories of Dougal Graham. It has escaped the attention of Burns's editors hitherto, but seems highly probable that Graham's best-known comic chapbook, *John Cheap The Chapman*, helped to suggest to the poet the names and characteristics of his two drinking cronies, Tam and Souter Johnny.

Douglas Graham's knockabout chapman hero, John, who has 'a hundred merry exploits', most of them involv-

ing escapes from situations into which his boldness leads
him, enjoys the friendship of a 'sticked shaver' called
'drouthy Tom'. They are both idle, and there is nothing
they like better than to find a sympathetic landlady, and
spend day after day drinking, without thought of the
reckoning. Dougal Graham is no Burns, but he conveys
vividly the idea of a protracted companionable drinking
session, for instance at the beginning of the second part of
John Cheap The Chapman

> We again came to a place near Sutry-hill where the
> ale was good, and very civil usage, and our draught
> being very great, the more we drank, the better we
> loved it

and again in the third and last part

> So I went to Linlithgow that night, where I met with
> Drouthy Tom my sweet and dear companion and
> here we held a most terrible encounter with the
> tippeny for two nights and a day.

This was taken up by the poet, and, along with his own
market-day experience and observation, supplied a hint
for his portrayal of sustained conviviality:

> . . . at his elbow, Souter *Johnny*,
> His ancient, trusty, drouthy crony;   thirsty
> *Tam* lo'ed him like a vera brither;   loved
> They had been fou for weeks thegither.

In the same way, Burns recalled in the central incident of
'Tam o' Shanter', and especially in the line

> Now, *Tam*, O *Tam*! had thae been queans

Dougal Graham's characterisation of Drouthy Tom as
one who, given half a chance, 'fell' a courting and a
kissing': in the case of Tam o' Shanter, a susceptibility to
female beauty is made unforgettable. Other details in the
chapbook were too broad to use, but nevertheless have a

connection with the poem. The chapbook ends with a
woman telling a story against a chapman:

> ane of them came by ae day, and sell'd our Meg twa
> ell and a quarter o' linen to be her bridal sark, for he
> had nae mair, and when she made it, and pat it on, it
> widna hide her hech, hech, hech, he.

The context in 'Tam o' Shanter' was not right for this jest
— which may have been traditional before Dougal
Graham dared to print it — but Burns slyly worked in a
comment on 'snaw-white seventeen hunder linnen', and
also the information that Nannie's garment had been
fashioned for her long years before she reached the
shapely maturity which held Tam's admiring gaze.

John Cheap the Chapman tells in unsubtle, rat-a-tat
manner of cheeky, ne'er-do-weel male escapades. In
'Tam o' Shanter', on the other hand, there is only one
adventurous encounter (if we except what happens to
Meg), at Alloway Kirk; but in the course of the poem all
human nature is illuminated. It is the difference between
the action-packed but one-dimensional world of the
chapbook or its lineal descendant, the illustrated comic,
and life itself. The reader, and still more the listener, is
made to feel that he has known Tam all his days, that he
knows him 'like a vera brither'. The appeal throughout is
to universal instincts and feelings; we share the hero's
moments of glory and of terror, understand what he is
going through, and feel relief along with him at the end.
'Tam o' Shanter' is Everyman, in his cheeful gregarious-
ness, in the 'blest insensibility' with which he rides
through the storm, whistling to keep his spirits up, in his
vulnerability, and in his resilience. The finest poetry is
always up to date, accommodating changing emphases.
What more modern lesson could there be for Tam than
that it is dangerous to treat Nannie — not to mention
Kate

Nursing her wrath to keep it warm

— as mere 'sex objects'? It is surely no more possible for today's orthodox than for their predecessors to condemn him. The poem works through acceptance, communicates a sense of tolerance, is open to life.

There is in Burns a readiness to accept erring human beings which distinguishes him from his eighteenth-century predecessor Pope and places him in the company of Chaucer.

Worthy of Chaucer, too, is the style of story-telling, apparently artless, but in reality a model of narrative tact and control. Near the beginning, Burns handles a contrast beloved of earlier Scottish poets, between the cosy scene indoors and the hostile world of nature outside; through original observation and mastery of the pace of the verse, he make it all his own. Particular care is shown in the choice of descriptive detail for what it contributes to the overall mood, not merely for the effect of individual images. Robert Ainslie noted, when Burns recited 'Tam o' Shanter' to him at Ellisland, that the passage conveying Tam's intimate comfort in the inn included the lines

> The crickets joined the chirping cry,
> The kittlin chased her tail for joy.   kitten

Fine though these lines are, Burns deleted them from the poem when published, no doubt because, as Scott surmised, he judged the transition from a glimpse of the behaviour of Tam, the landlord, and the landlord's wife to 'little circumstances' a lapse. Similarly, he strengthened the tonal unity of the scene in which Tam is confronted by horrific objects at Kirk-Alloway by omitting a satiric hit at a lawyer and a priest. This was done on the advice of a critic, A. F. Tytler. Tytler praised the 'horrible fancy' of this part of the poem, but suggested that the lines

> Three Lawyers' tongues, turn'd inside
> out,
patch   Wi' lies seam'd like a beggar's clout;
> Three Priests' hearts, rotten, black as
> muck,
corner   Lay stinking, vile, in every neuk

'though good in themselves, yet, as they derive all their merit from the satire they contain, are here rather misplaced among the circumstances of pure horror'.[12] It was not often that Burns was offered intelligent criticism, and he readily accepted it in this instance. While 'Tam o' Shanter' offers a succession of varied pictures, and the tone alters along with them, nothing is allowed to impede the onward flow of the tale. At this point in the poem, Burns is intent on creating a particular kind of outlandish Gothic atmosphere; much 'o' horrible and aweful'' has a place, but not the kind of professional satire which belonged in 'Death and Doctor Hornbook'.

A great deal depends upon the convincing quality of the 'voice' which recounts all that happens to Tam. The narrator is at once detached from the hero, being ready to comment knowingly on his weaknesses, and capable of identifying with Tam's unrespectable viewpoint:

> But wither'd beldams, auld and droll,
withered wean   Rigwoodie hags wad spean a foal,
leaping crook Lowping and flinging on a crummock
> I wonder didna turn thy stomach.

It is this flexibility of manner, and constantly varying degree of obliquity in narrative, which makes it possible for Burns to include so wide a range of ironical reference. The same voice which exclaims in a corner of the inn

> I wonder didna turn thy stomach

muses as if in mixed company, but still for the amusement of his own sex,

Ah, gentle dames! it gars me greet,   makes   weep
To think how many counsels sweet,
How mony lengthen'd sage advices,
The husband frae the wife despises!

Drollery is pervasive, yet a balance is maintained between such asides, with their glancing connection with the theme of the war of the sexes, and the story itself.

Interestingly, A. F. Tytler found fault with the end of the poem, writing to Burns:

> the winding-up, or conclusion, of the story is not commensurate to the interest which is excited by the descriptive and characteristic painting of the preceding parts. The preparation is fine, but the result is not adequate. But for this, perhaps, you have a good apology — you stick to the popular tale.

The poet replied in tactful words which perhaps indicate that he believed there was at least a grain of truth in the criticism:

> as to the falling off in the catastrophe, for the reason you justly adduce, it cannot easily be remedied.

He might have added that the incident of Meg's tail was calculated to keep everyone guessing, however abruptly the poem might be thought to end. Not for him the charge that he had been guilty of not knowing when to stop.

NOTES

1. *Ayrshire At the Time of Burns,* ed. John Strawhorn, Ayrshire Archaeological and Natural History Society Collection, v, 1959, p. 78.
2. The words are those of Robert Heron. Cf. *Robert Burns: The Critical Heritage,* ed. D. A. Low, 1974, p. 15.
3. I wish to thank the Editor of the *Burns Chronicle* for allowing me to reprint, with minor changes, my discussion of 'Death and Doctor Hornbook' in the *Burns Chronicle* of 1973.
4. *Poems and Songs of Robert Burns,* ed. James Kinsley, 1968, 84.

5. *Letters of Robert Burns*, I, 135.
6. Quoted in Kinsley, III, 1053.
7. *Robert Burns: The Critical Heritage*, pp. 286-7.
8. L. G. Gibbon, *Sunset Song*, ed. J. T. Low, 1971, p. 15.
9. *Letters of Robert Burns*, I, 423.
10. Quoted in Kinsley, III, 1347-8.
11. *Letters of Robert Burns*, II, 30-31.
12. *Robert Burns: The Critical Heritage*, pp. 95-6.

CHAPTER 5

SONG

Song-writing was an early interest of Burns, one which grew steadily as his life went on. In his later years he became so deeply involved in the collecting, editing, and writing of songs that he made many jokes about his hobby. Burns had first hand knowledge and an instinctive love of traditional tunes, coupled with an aptitude for matching words to them. Along with this basic understanding went a wish to bring together as many of the fine melodies of Scotland as he could and to supply them with appropriate words. Especially after he had begun to collaborate with James Johnson on *The Scots Musical Museum* in 1787, he saw his role as 'Scotia's bard' increasingly in terms of song-collecting. He thought about song in social terms, and wanted to give back to the Scottish people in the best form possible what he conceived to belong to them, namely a heritage of fine tunes and accompanying words. His purpose could be described as part poetic, part musical, and part antiquarian. Fundamentally, he was obeying artistic and patriotic instinct.

Song differs from melody as such in that it requires words and the voice for completeness. Burns believed that by adding words to melody it ought to be possible to release the full expressive potential within the tunes of his native land. Verses were needed to convey the sentiment or quality of feeling which a good tune often suggested to him, but which could be fully articulated only through a combination of melody and words. Equally, he took the view that to verse which otherwise might exist only at the

H

level of writing, and not be uttered, music added a fresh dimension, and with it the exciting communicative possibility of actual performance.

It often goes unrecognised that Burns as song-writer is no less an artist working in two related media than is his English contemporary the poet and visual artist Blake. Formally, the two differ in that Burns matches his words to pre-existent tunes, whereas Blake creates both verbal and visual images; but the kinship remains between Burns's combined communicative form and that practised by Blake in, say, *Songs Of Innocence and Experience*. It is necessary to take into account the tunes for which Burns wrote, as well as his verses, just as it is essential to consider along with the words of Blake's lyrics their accompanying pictorial designs. A song can be experienced as a whole only when it is sung. Reading the words on the page in isolation from the tune — or for that matter the musical notes apart from the words — is better than nothing, but it may often be misleading. In particular, it cannot do justice to the way in which a good tune has been enhanced by verses which work in performance because they match the melodic character simply and appropriately.

In an interleaved copy of *The Scots Musical Museum* Burns commented, 'Here, once for all, let me apologise for many silly compositions of mine in this work. Many beautiful airs wanted words; in the hurry of other avocations, if I could string a parcel of rhymes together any thing near tolerable, I was fain to let them pass. He must be an excellent poet indeed, whose every performance is excellent'.[1] Similarly, he wrote to George Thomson in September 1794, 'I think that it is better to have mediocre verses to a favourite air than none at all. — On this principle I have all along proceeded in the Scots Musical Museum'.[2] The principle involves treating a song as words created for a particular tune. One implica-

tion of Burns's self-critical awareness is obvious. We do
much better to pay attention to how his songs operate in
terms of his own stated purpose, than to treat them as
though they were *poems* submitted for publication apart
from their tunes. A surprisingly large number do in fact
stand out poetically in their own right as words on the
page, but they were not conceived with this in mind, and
it is certainly a mistake to dismiss too quickly and without
listening to a performance words which, on their own,
may appear rough and ready.

Among the songs which predate the Kilmarnock
edition, the much anthologised 'Mary Morison' is an
example of the kind which both performs well and reads
well. Hugh MacDiarmid, whose attitude to Burns was
inevitably that of rival in Scottish poetry as well as
successor, commented intriguingly on 'the supreme
power of Burns's finest line,

"ye are na Mary Morison"'.[3]   you   not

He perhaps had in mind Burns's 'voice', the mastery of
idiom in his use of colloquial speech to express deep
feeling. What distinguishes the song in its entirety is the
apt combination of images of sight and sound ('Yestreen
when to the trembling string/ the dance gaed through the
lighted ha') with direct personal statement and a mood of
wistful tenderness:

O Mary, at thy window be,
   It is the wish'd, the trysted hour;   appointed
Those smiles and glances let me see,
   That makes the miser's treasure poor:
How blythely wad I bide the stoure,   endure dust
   A weary slave frae sun to sun;   from
Could I the rich reward secure,
   The lovely Mary Morison!

yesterday evening	Yestreen when to the trembling string
	The dance gaed through the lighted
went hall	ha',
	To thee my fancy took its wing,
	I sat, but neither heard, nor saw:
fine-looking	Though this was fair, and that was braw,
that all	And yon the toast of a' the town,
	I sigh'd, and said amang them a',
	'Ye are na Mary Morison'.
	O Mary, canst thou wreck his peace,
who would	Wha for thy sake wad gladly die!
	Or canst thou break that heart of his,
fault	Whase only faute is loving thee!
give	If love for love thou wilt na gie,
	At least be pity to me shown;
cannot	A thought ungentle canna be
	The thought o' Mary Morison.

It is clear that, even while writing his lovesong, Burns has kept in mind the constraints imposed by a tune he knows well, the Scots reel 'Duncan Davison'. So familiar with it is he that he has been able to put its very strict pattern to original use. James Kinsley notes about 'Mary Morison', 'as a *song*, it is a notable early attempt to marry words to music. The air breaks conventionally at the end of the first part; but over it Burns constructs a stanza of eight phrases, crossing and binding the two parts together with the rhyme repeating in the second, fourth, fifth, and seventh lines to confirm the unity of the stanza and the air. The song opens sedately, on a low note; but at the fifth line, where the reel breaks and lifts, conventional address is intensified into passionate declaration, 'expressing' the discovered character of the tune'.[4]

'Mary Morison' is a unified love-lyric of a type rare in any language: it illustrates Stendhal's view that 'Burns was more than half a musician'. A great deal flowed from his early familiarity with the types of tune — reels, jigs, and strathspeys — which he made his own in song-writing. Although strathspeys gave him 'exquisite pleasure', reels outnumbered the rest. From such early songs as 'Tibbie, I hae seen the day', which exploits the tune 'Invercauld's Reel' to poke derisive fun at a girl with her nose in the air

But Tibby lass tak' my advice	take
Your daddie's gear mak's you sae nice	property makes
The de'il a ane wad speir your price	not a single one would
Were ye as poor as I	

until the end of his career, Burns was an enthusiast for supplying good reels with original words. Quite often, he would return to a favourite air and re-use it in a completely new way. He twice set words, for example, to the traditional reel 'For a' that an' a' that' which inspired the Bard's song in 'Love and Liberty'. In the cantata, the song is an ironic one communicating the essentially disrespectful, libertine outlook of a maker of rhymes who will have no truck with polite pretensions about poetry, but who prefers instead to drink and make love to 'the Fair':

I am a bard of no regard,	
Wi' gentle folks an' a' that:	all
But HOMER LIKE the glowran byke,	staring crowd
Frae town to town I draw that.	from

Chorus —

For a' that an' a' that,	
An' twice as muckle's a' that,	much
I've lost but ANE, I've TWA behin'.	one two
I've WIFE ENEUGH for a' that.	enough

I never drank the Muses' STANK	pool of standing water
Castalia's burn an' a' that,	
But there it streams an' richly reams,	froths
My HELICON I ca' that.	
For a' that &c.	

Great love I bear to all the FAIR,
    Their humble slave an' a' that;
But lordly WILL, I hold it still
frustrate   A mortal sin to thraw that.
      For a' that &c.

In raptures sweet this hour we meet,
    Wi' mutual love an' a' that;
flyBut for how lang the FLIE MAY
sting   STANG,
    Let INCLINATION law that.
      For a' that &c.

The defiant character of the same tune suggested a quite different set of ideas some years later when, inspired by Tom Paine's *The Rights Of Man* and the French Revolution, Burns wrote a political song destined to become internationally famous and, as one editor puts it, to occupy 'a central place in the psalmody of radicalism'. He sent this song to George Thomson in January 1795 with the comment, 'A great critic, Aiken on songs, says that love and wine are the exclusive themes for song-writing, — The following is on neither subject. . . .'[5] What the new song shares with the Bard's song in 'Love and Liberty' is fidelity to the spirit of attack in its tune — which in that sense is Burns's inspiration — and a correspondingly bold and direct use of Scots. There is no compromise here, no concession to gentility, any more than in 'Love and Liberty'; only this time, the song reaches out to the 'real' world of politics to assert the worth of all poor and underprivileged people:

Is there, for honest poverty
hangs   That hings his head, and a' that:
The coward-slave, we pass him by,
    We dare be poor for a' that!

For a' that, and a' that,
   Our toils obscure, and a' that,
The rank is but the guinea's stamp,
   The Man's the gowd for a' that. —   *gold*
What though on hamely fare we dine,   *homely*
   Wear hoddin grey, and a' that.   *rough   homespun*
Gie fools their silks, and knaves their
     wine,   *give*
   A Man's a Man for a' that.
  For a' that, and a' that,
   Their tinsel show, and a' that;
  The honest man, though e'er sae poor,   *ever*
   Is king o' men for a' that. —
Ye see yon birkie ca'd, a lord,   *fellow*
   Wha struts, and stares, and a' that,
Though hundreds worship at his word,
   He's but a coof for a' that.   *fool*
  For a' that, and a' that,
   His ribband, star and a' that,
  The man of independant mind,
   He looks and laughs at a' that. —

A prince can mak a belted knight,
   A marquis, duke, and a' that;
But an honest man's aboon his might,   *above*
   Gude faith he mauna fa' that!   *must not   lay claim to*
  For a' that, and a' that,
   Their dignities, and a' that,
  The pith o' Sense, and pride o' Worth,
   Are higher rank than a' that. —
Then let us pray that come it may,
   As come it will for a' that,
That Sense and Worth, o'er a' the earth
   Shall bear the gree, and a' that.   *come off best*
  For a' that, and a' that,
   It's comin yet for a' that,
  That Man to Man the warld o'er,
   Shall brothers be for a' that. —

'A man's a man' shares with all of Burns's best work, whether in poetry or song, a natural sounding and convincing idiom. The basis, as in 'The Twa Dogs', is such complete control over spoken utterance as to make art conceal art. To this authenticity of speech, Burns adds a gift of timing and insight into the phrasing of the music. Thus in line two, 'hings his head' is spoken — and sung — in a single emphatic phrase, and becomes an indicator of inner contempt which is directed primarily at those who cause such false thinking and behaviour on the part of any poor man. The songwriter makes use both of easily understood English

> The coward-slave, we pass him by

and of Scots forms which betoken social solidarity, and which are sometimes, by intention, powerfully reductive:

> Ye see yon birkie ca'd a lord,
>> Wha struts, and stares, and a' that.

Structurally, the song accumulates energy and feeling as it goes on — had he not learned how to capitalise on this aspect of the melody in the Bard's song in 'Love and Liberty'? — so that, by the time the final stanza is reached, Burns is in a position to draw together the implications of the social criticisms already made, and to announce an all inclusive message of revolutionary brotherhood:

> Then let us pray that come it may,
>> As come it will for a' that,
> That Sense and Worth, o'er a' the earth

come off best
>> Shall bear the gree, and a' that.
> For a' that, and a' that,
>> It's comin yet for a' that,
> That Man to Man the warld o'er,
>> Shall brothers be for a' that.

In the mid 1790s the obstacles to revolutionary change were large, and they were themselves subject to change all the time. The three words 'for a' that' are Burns's signature on this song. His swift mind has seen that despite everything adverse, change must come. In looking towards the future and confronting difficulty, shared beliefs and hopes count for more than the details of argument and counter-argument. Hence 'it's comin yet for a' that'.

An extempore (tune title unrecorded) written in a moment of wry self-assessment when he was twenty-three shows Burns's instinct for expressing his feelings in song directly and with humour:

> O why the deuce should I repine,
>   And be an ill foreboder;
> I'm twenty-three, and five feet nine,
>   I'll go and be a sodger.   soldier
> I gat some gear wi' meikle care,   got money much
>   I held it weel thegither;   well
> But now its gane, and something mair,   gone more
>   I'll go and be a sodger.

In 1794 Burns wrote another song about himself which in his own judgement gives an accurate portrait of his mind. To the traditional air 'Lumps o' puddins' he composed this set of words:

> Contented wi' little, and cantie wi' mair,   cheerful more
> Whene'er I forgather wi' Sorrow and
>   Care,
> I gie them a skelp, as they're creeping   slap
>   alang,   along
> Wi' a cog o' gude swats and an auld   measure small beer
>   Scotish sang.
>
> I whyles claw the elbow o' troublesome   sometimes
>   thought;
> But Man is a soger, and Life is a faught: soldier fight
> My mirth and gude humour are coin in
>   my pouch,
> And my FREEDOM's my Lairdship nae
>   monarch dare touch.

A towmond o' trouble, should they be my
year lot   fa',
patches up all   A night o' gude fellowship sowthers it a';
When at the blythe end of our journey at
last,
devil   Wha the deil ever thinks o' the road he
has past.

Blind Chance, let her snapper and stoyte
stumble stagger   on her way;
Be't to me, be't frae me, e'n let the jade
be it wench go   gae:
Come Ease, or come Travail; come
Pleasure, or Pain;
My warst word is — 'Welcome and
worst   welcome again!'

The happy-go-lucky philosophy which 'Contented wi'
little, an cantie wi' mair' expresses underlines Burns's
belief in song as a social art. He responded positively to
any exchange of words and melodies with friends; and
was ready to exercise his skill with words if by doing so he
could entertain his companions. In this connection, there
is special interest in a drinking-song he wrote to a tune
composed by his friend Alan Masterton. Usually, Burns
drew his inspiration from tunes which had been in circula-
tion for many years, but 'Willie brew'd a peck o' maut'
shows that he was ready to make an exception in response
to the right stimulus.

In November 1794 he wrote to George Thomson,
'Scots Bacchanalians we certainly want, though the few
that we have are excellent'.[6] The air of 'Willie brew'd a
peck o' maut', he noted, 'is Masterton's; the song mine.
The occasion of it was this. — Mr Wm Nicol, of the High
School, Edinr, during the autumn vacation being at
Moffat, honest Allan, who was at that time on a visit to
Dalswinton, and I went to pay Nicol a visit. We had such

a joyous meeting that Mr Masterton and I each in our own way should celebrate the business'.[7] Masterton was a practised composer of song tunes, and he rose to the occasion. In his song Burns catches the mood of the evening to perfection, using the chorus for what David Daiches has described as 'sublime understatement' and matching the lifts and runs of Masterton's air as he does so:

O Willie brew'd a peck o' maut,	malt
And Rob and Allan cam to see;	
Three blyther hearts, that lee lang night,	whole
Ye wad na found in Christendie.	not have Christendom.

Chorus

We are na fou, we're nae that fou,	not drunk
But just a drappie in our e'e;	little drop
The cock may craw, the day may daw,	crow dawn
And aye we'll taste the barley bree.	whisky

Here are we met, three merry boys,
    Three merry boys I trow are we;
And mony a night we've merry been,
    And mony a night we hope to be!
    Chos. We are na fou, &c.

It is the moon, I ken her horn,	know
That's blinkin in the lift sae hie;	sky high
She shines sae bright to wyle us hame,	home
But by my sooth she'll wait a wee!	little
Chos. We are na fou, &c.	

Wha first shall rise to gang awa,	go away
A cuckold, coward loun is he!	rogue
Wha first beside his chair shall fa',	fall
He is the king amang us three!	
Chos. We are na fou, &c.	

Burns conceived of his role as writer, mender, and editor

of songs for James Johnson's *Scots Musical Museum* as that of someone contributing to the live song culture of Scotland. 'Museum' means 'temple of the Muses'; there was in Burns's eyes nothing dusty or obscurantist about the undertaking. Rather, the emphasis was on making songs available in their authentic simplicity, without elaborate musical arrangement. Each volume of the *Museum* carries on its title-page a statement declaring 'In this publication the original simplicity of our Ancient National Airs is retained unincumbered with useless Accompaniments & graces depriving the hearers of the sweet simplicity of their native melodies'. Burns's responsibility was to collect and make use of as many of the old words and traditional choruses as possible, and where these were unavailable to supply appropriate new words, written by others or by himself.

During the first year of his collaboration with Johnson Burns wrote enthusiastically to a number of correspondents about the *Scots Musical Museum* project. A brief selection of his remarks to different friends illustrates how excited he felt to be involved in a publishing enterprise which was so close to his interests:

> An engraver, James Johnson . . . has, not from mercenary views but from an honest Scotch enthusiasm, set about collecting all our native Songs . . . and Dr Beattie and Blacklock, Mr Tytler, Woodhouseleee, and your humble servant to the utmost of his small power, assist in collecting the old poetry, or sometimes to a fine air to make a stanza, when it has no words . . .
>
> I have been absolutely crazed about it, collecting old stanzas, and every information remaining respecting their origin, authors, &c . . .
>
> This, you will easily guess, is an undertaking exactly to my taste. — I have collected, begg'd, borrow'd and stolen all the songs I could meet with . . .

I invariably hold it sacriledge to add anything of
my own to help out with the shatter'd wrecks of these
venerable old compositions; but they have many
various readings . . .

The world may think slightingly of the craft of
song-making, if they please, but, as Job says, — 'O
that mine adversary had written a book!' — let them
try. There is a certain something in the old Scotch
songs, a wild happiness of thought and expression
which peculiarly marks them, not only from English
songs, but also from the modern efforts of song-
wrights, in our native manner and language.[8]

The truth of this last statement can be tested, as it
happens, by setting beside a traditional Scots song a song
which Burns himself was tempted to write in a playful
spirit of emulation. He had written to Mrs Dunlop in
March 1787,

Scottish scenes, and Scottish story are the themes I
could wish to sing. — I have no greater, no dearer
aim than to have it in my power, unplagu'd with the
routine of business, for which Heaven knows I am
unfit enough, to make leisurely pilgrimages through
Caledonia; to sit on the fields of her battles; to
wander on the romantic banks of her rivers; and to
muse by the stately tower or venerable ruins, once the
honored abodes of her heroes.[9]

In practice, it was relatively seldom that Burns responded
to places by writing about them immediately while on the
spot. More often, he stored up images in his mind and
returned to them later. At the Falls of Aberfeldy,
however, he found himself remembering a well-known
love 'debate' in a song from north-eastern Scotland, 'The
Birks of Abergeldie':

                    Bonny lassie, will ye go,
                        Will ye go, will ye go,
                    Bonny lassie, will ye go
birches   To the birks o' Abergeldie?
                    Ye shall get a gown of silk
                        A gown of silk, a gown of silk,
                    Ye shall get a gown of silk,
glossy woollen stuff woven with satin   And a coat of calimancoe.
not go   No, kind Sir, I dare nae gang,
                        I dare nae gang, I dare nae gang
                    Na, kind Sir, I dare nae gang,
mother   My minnie she'll be angry.
sorely would scold Sair, sair wad she flyte,
                        Wad she flyte, wad she flyte,
                    Sair, sair wad she flyte,
curse   And sair wad she ban me.[10]

With the insistent tune 'The birks of Abergeldie' running
in his head, Burns decided to pay tribute to the beauty of
the Perthshire waterfall by making up verses of his own
there and then. The song of courtship which resulted was
published in *The Scots Musical Museum* along with the traditional words. It has since taken the place of the original
'Birks of Abergeldie' as a popular favourite, which is
arguably not an improvement, as Burns writes here in a
consciously stylised manner which is a little too close to
drawing-room song convention to represent him at his
best:

                    Bonny lassie, will ye go, will ye go, will
                        ye go;
                    Bonny lassie, will ye go to the birks of
                        Aberfeldy.

                                    I

hillsides   Now Simmer blinks on flowery braes,
                    And o'er the chrystal streamlets plays;
                    Come let us spend the lightsome days
                        In the birks of Aberfeldy.

Bonny lassie, will ye go, will ye go, will
      ye go,
Bonny lassie, will ye go to the birks of
      Aberfeldy.

II

The little birdies blythely sing,
Whiles o'er their heads the hazels hing;   hang
Or lightly flit on wanton wing
    In the birks of Aberfeldy.
Bonny lassie, &c.

III

The braes ascend like lofty wa's,   walls
The foamy stream deep-roaring fa's,   falls
O'er-hung wi' fragrant-spreading shaws,   woods
    The birks of Aberfeldy.
Bonny lassie, &c.

IV

The hoary cliffs are crowned wi' flowers,
White o'er the linns the burnie pours,   waterfall stream
And rising weets wi' misty showers   wets
    The birks of Aberfeldy.
Bonny lassie, &c.

V

Let Fortune's gifts at random flee,
They ne'er shall draw a wish frae me;
Supremely blest wi' love and thee
    In the birks of Aberfeldy.
Bonny lassie, &c.

Often, Burns found himself with little to work on but the
first verse or chorus of an old song. His record of success
in 'patching' or restoring songs for Johnson on the basis

of inadequate fragments handed down from the past is outstanding. In many instances he creates what is essentially a new song from little more than a hint supplied by tradition. His invariable starting-point was the tune. In a letter commenting on the tune 'Laddie, lie near me', he describes what became his habitual method in the writing of songs:

> untill I am compleat master of a tune, in my own singing, (such as it is) I never can compose for it. — My way is: I consider the poetic Sentiment, correspondent to my idea of the musical expression; then chuse my theme; begin one Stanza; when that is composed, which is generally the most difficult part of the business, I walk out, sit down now & then, look out for objects in Nature around me that are in unison or harmony with the cogitations of my fancy & workings of my bosom; humming every now & then the air with the verses I have framed: when I feel my Muse beginning to jade, I retire to the solitary fireside of my study, & there commit my effusions to paper; swinging, at intervals, on the hind-legs of my elbow-chair, by way of calling forth my own critical strictures, as my pen goes on.[11]

A justly famous song, 'O whistle, an' I'll come to you, my lad' illustrates that on occasion Burns returned after a period of years to develop a theme which he had left incomplete. In the second volume of *The Scots Musical Museum* in 1788 he printed two stanzas, the first of which was traditional, the second his own:

> O whistle, an' I'll come to you, my lad;
> O whistle, an' I'll come to you, my lad:
> Though father and mither should baith
>   gae mad,
> O whistle, an' I'll come to you, my lad.

both
go

Come down the back stairs when ye come
    to court me;
Come down the back stairs when ye come
    to court me:
Come down the back stairs, and let
    naebody see;   *nobody*
And come as ye were na' coming to me.   *as if not*

Then in 1793 Burns sent to George Thomson an
expanded verson of the song in which he took much
further his characterisation of the girl addressing her
lover. In the later version her attitude remains playful and
affectionate, but she has now become more vulnerable
than before, partly through the jealousy to which she
owns in the final stanza:

O whistle, and I'll come to ye, my lad,
O whistle, and I'll come to ye, my lad;
Tho' father, and mother, and a' should
    gae mad,
    Thy Jeanie will venture wi' ye, my lad.

But warily tent, when ye come to court   *take care*
    me,
And come nae unless the back-yett be
    a-jee;   *back gate   ajar*
Syne up the back-style and let naebody
    see,   *back stile*
    And come as ye were na coming to me
    — —

    And come as ye were na coming to me
    — —

    O whistle &c.

At kirk, or at market whene'er ye meet   *church*
    me,
Gang by me as tho' that ye car'd nae a
    flie;   *go   not a fly*

I

But steal me a blink o' your bonie black
eye   e'e,
    Yet look as ye were na looking at me
as if   — —
    Yet look as ye were na looking at me
       — —
    O whistle &c.

    Ay vow and protest that ye care na for
      me,
slight a   And whyles ye may lightly my beauty a
little   wee;
not another But court nae anither, tho' jokin ye be,
lure   For fear that she wyle your fancy frae
      me — —
      For fear that she wyle your fancy frae
      me.

What counts for most in song is that there should be a
fusion between the verbal and musical content. The first
essential is that the mood and spirit of the tune should in
some way be caught, embodied, and mirrored in the
words going along with it. The guiding idea with Burns's
work for Johnson — as so often in the art of the eighteenth
century — is that of appropriateness or 'decorum'. In
song after song his writing displays exceptional flair and
tact. Time and again, whether or not his words are
memorable, they are adapted to their melody.

    Inevitably, such a claim leads us into subjective
considerations of how closely particular tunes and verses
suit and complement each other. But while opinions may
differ about the quality of individual examples of the
song-writer's craft, one reason for Burns's overall
achievement in song can be identified with confidence.
He was very much the product of his age and society in
valuing 'sentiment' as the verbal language suited to song.
If we look at a selection of the songs he supplied for
volume 4 of the *Scots Musical Museum*, published in 1792,

his approach is seen to be consistent. He did not tire of paying compliments in verse with a melody in mind. In this process, the melody and the girl belonged together. Nor did he think it artificial to express devotion to his native land in song. However often he found himself obliging James Johnson, his personal and patriotic feelings remained strong. Sentiment was verbalised feeling, and sentiment and song went together as part of a unity which included both.

'Now westlin winds, and slaught'ring guns' was drafted when Burns was in love with Peggy Thomson at the age of seventeen. Interestingly, this song was originally an English composition. Only when he was looking for material for volume 4 of the *Museum* did Burns partly recast it in Scots. In the first version, the winds are 'breezy', not westlin; the bird in line three is the 'moorcock' rather than the gorcock; line 9 reads

The Partridge loves the fruitful fells

instead of

The Pairtick lo'es the fruitfu' fells;

and there are other minor differences in diction. Yet the sentiment in stanzas three and four is unchanged in the *Scots Musical Museum* copy. The song-writer at this point is concerned to show that he shares a sense of belonging to 'general' nature. It is quite natural for him to choose English as the language of moral and social reflection in stanza three, where he introduces a note of protest against the 'slaught'ring guns' (originally 'sportsmen's guns') of the opening line.

Thus ev'ry kind their pleasure find,
    The savage and the tender;
Some social join, and leagues combine;
    Some solitary wander:

> Avaunt, away! the cruel sway,
>   Tyrannic man's dominion;
> The Sportsman's joy, the murdring cry,
>   The flutt'ring, gory pinion!

English having been used so uncompromisingly here, decorum suggests that the final stanza should contain no more than a hint of Scots phrasing, in 'o' for the original 'of' (line 30), and 'ilka' for 'ev'ry' (last line).

Practice makes perfect. Another song published in the fourth volume of the *Museum* which illustrates the full meaning of sentiment, and also its marriage to melody, is 'Ae fond kiss', perhaps the most famous of all Burns's love-lyrics, with its unforgettable fourth stanza:

> Had we never lov'd sae kindly,
> Had we never lov'd sae blindly,
> Never met — or never parted,
> We had ne'er been broken-hearted.

These words, containing as Scott put it 'the essence of a thousand love tales', are a distillation of feeling in keeping with the Gaelic melody 'Rory Dall's port' which Burns had in mind. In sending Clarinda a number of his songs, he commented, 'I have just been composing to different tunes, for the Collection of Songs of which you have three volumes, and of which you shall have the fourth'.

'Ae fond kiss' is a supreme expression of strong personal sentiment for a named individual of the opposite sex. It ends on a note of anguished conflict:

> Warring sighs and groans I'll wage thee.

In a quite different way, a tranquil song like ''O leeze me on my Spinning-Wheel' also conveys what Burns's age would have called sentiment — in this instance a graceful tribute in response to the pastoral appeal of life set in natural surroundings, free from worldly concerns. Verse

by verse, the song creates awareness that beauty and simplicity are an integral part of Bessy's character, no less
than of the world of nature. The life of Bessy with her
spinning wheel — a life which is 'simple' in the best sense,
selected features of external nature, and the rippling
melody all fuse together in Burns's treatment. The
cumulative effect of a build-up of melody and words is
such that Burns is able without too obvious a transition to
use the final stanza to express a characteristic social
criticism:

Wi' sma' to sell, and less to buy,	little
Aboon distress, below envy,	above
O wha wad leave this humble state,	who would
For a' the pride of a' the Great?	all
Amid their flairing, idle toys,	gaudy
Amid their cumbrous, dinsome joys,	noisy
Can they the peace and pleasure feel	
Of Bessy at her spinnin wheel!	

Just as in 'Ae fond kiss' he gives new meaning and
passion to the expected sentiment of lovesong, so in this
song he deepens and naturalises the idiom of feeling
which marks eighteenth-century pastoral verse.

Burns had always felt strongly about favourite places,
and was a lover of running water. 'Afton Water' cele-
brates a well-loved scene, in a manner which is
thoroughly characteristic of the song-writer. The
distinguishing mark of the song is once more a
remarkable unity between words and melody. A song of
this type is likely to strike the listener as a highly
successful attempt to verbalise or express the character of
the tune, as well as of a particular scene and love
situation. The poet wishes to sing in praise of the river
because he is happy and his heart is full. Accordingly, he
allows his thoughts to follow the gentle curve of a tune he
knows well.

> Flow gently, sweet Afton, among thy
>   green braes,
> Flow gently, I'll sing thee a song in thy
>   praise;
> My Mary's asleep by thy murmuring
>   stream,
> Flow gently, sweet Afton, disturb not her
>   dream!

The words are mostly English, yet have a sprinkling of Scots: braes, glen, birk. This is often the diction Burns chooses when he is seeking to convey tender and romantically exalted sentiment.

We notice an intensification of Scots forms in 'Ye banks and braes of bonie Doon'. The fact that this is a song of unhappy love and agitated feeling perhaps helps to explain the use of a larger number of Scots words; but it is of interest also that the song contains such unmodified English lines as

> That wantons thro' the flowering thorn

and

> Departed never to return!

which ensure that there is an identifiable element of 'pure' sentiment along with the personal accent of distress.

In writing 'Such a parcel of rogues in a nation', Burns was building on inherited example. The events of the period leading up to the Union of the Parliaments in 1707 had seared themselves into the nation's memory, to a degree which would be rivalled in the next century only by the shock of the Highland Clearances. Where Burns is exceptional is in his responsiveness not only to the political ideas but to the feelings of those Scots who felt betrayed by the Act of Union. His song is one of outraged national pride, and of a bitter resignation. He puts